Let the Light Shine

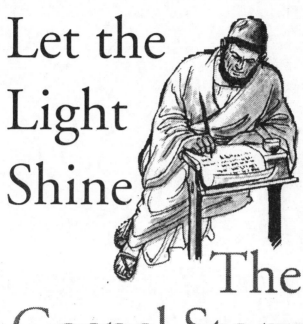

The Gospel Story for young people

Flor McCarthy SDB

VERITAS

Published 1994 by
Veritas Publications
7-8 Lower Abbey Street
Dublin 1

First published 1982 by
Kairos Publications

ISBN 1 85390 242 X

British Library Cataloguing
in Publication Data.
A catalogue record for
this book is available
from the British Library.

Design: Bill Bolger
Cover illustration: Don Sutton International Photo Library
Illustrations: Copyright Les Editions du Bosquet/Fr Patrick Rogers CP
Printed in the Republic of Ireland by Criterion Press Ltd, Dublin

Contents

Introduction	7
Preparing the way for the Lord	9
Jesus appears on the scene	10
Clashing with Satan	11
Making friends	12
Showing his power	13
Beginning to preach	14
Some fishermen get hooked	15
A devil in the house of God	15
No rest for the good	16
Chatting at a well	17
The man who came in from the cold	19
The man who was let down by his friends	20
A tax collector joins	21
Watching like hawks	22
A night-time visitor	23
Picking his team	24
Sermon on a hill	25
A soldier's faith	29
Stopped on the way to the graveyard	30
Gate-crashing the party	31
A day of story-telling	32
Storm on the lake	35
Madman at large!	36
Who touched me?	37
Why is everybody crying?	38
Thrown out of his own village	39
Death of John the Baptist	40
An unplanned picnic	42
Saved from drowning	43
Another kind of food	44
The woman who refused to take no for an answer	45
Jesus sends out the Twelve	46
The lost sheep	47
The lost son	47
It's the inside that matters	49
How not to pray	50
No figs for the fig rolls	50
Kids' stuff	51
The man who could show no pity	52
On the mountain	53
Taking the road to Jerusalem	54

The man who came back to say thanks   54
Fire from heaven   55
Jobs for the boys   56
How to pray   57
It's dangerous to be rich   58
The rich fool   59
Rich man, poor man   59
Feathering your nest   61
Getting a bird's-eye view   62
The grape-pickers   63
A true neighbour   64
Stone throwing   65
Getting mud in the eye   66
The good shepherd   68
A narrow escape   69
Three loyal friends   70
The raising of Lazarus   70
No one ever spoke like this   72
Kicking up a stink about perfume   73
Palm Sunday demonstration   74
Aggro in God's house   75
The guests who failed to show up   76
Paying taxes to Caesar   77
A widow's mighty mite   77
The destruction of Jerusalem foretold   78
Do not be afraid   78
The talents   79
The Last Judgement   80
The calm before the storm   81
The Last Supper   81
The washing of the feet   82
Talking about the traitor   83
Instituting the Eucharist   84
A new commandment   84
Peter's denial foretold   84
Breaking up is never easy   85
I will not leave you orphans   85
The agony in the garden   86
The arrest   87
Trial before Annas   88
Before Caiphas and the council   89
Peter's denials   89
Judas ends it all   90
Trial before Pilate   91

Before Herod   92
Before Pilate again   92
The death sentence   93
Journey to Skull Hill   94
The Crucifixion   95
Jesus is mocked   95
Darkness at noon   96
The burial   97
Sad Saturday   98
An empty tomb   98
He's alive!   99
Crying by the tomb   99
The guards who ran away   100
Journey to Emmaus   100
Behind closed doors   102
The mark of the nails   102
Fish for breakfast   103
Last instructions and goodbye   105
Picking a sub for Judas   105
Wind and fire   106
Friends, lend me your ears   107
A new way of living   108
Those feet were meant for walking   108
Stop this preaching, or else!   109
Arrested again   110
The first deacons   111
The first martyr   111
Seeing the light   112
The end of the beginning   114
Appendix: Maps
1. Palestine in the Time of Christ   117
2. Jerusalem in the Time of Christ   118
3. The Mediterranean   119

Introduction

Practically everything in the Gospel is story. There are the stories which tell of things that happened to Jesus. There are the stories of encounters he had with different people. There are the stories of miracles he performed. And of course there are the stories he told as part of his teaching. The Gospel consists of a series of stories, but all of these coalesce to form one great story. The four Gospels are but four versions of the one story. That story is the Story of Jesus.

While we all like to listen to a story, we grow tired if we are told the same story over and over again. When that happens we switch off. We may be listening, but we aren't hearing. The same thing can happen with the Gospel Story. It may come across as old, stale and lifeless. Some have listened to it so many times that they no longer hear it.

The Gospel is the greatest story ever told. But we need to tell it in a way that appeals and gets through. We need to restore the wonder of it. We must release the energy contained in it, and harness the power it has to charm, surprise, shock, challenge and inspire all who hear it.

The Gospel text as it stands doesn't help. In spite of attempts at modernising the language, I believe it still doesn't speak clearly, especially to the young. It doesn't come alive. The stories are related all too briefly, and far too much background information is taken for granted.

We need to bring the story to life. We need to dress it up in a new language so that it will sound fresh and speak in the present tense. We need to tell it in such a way that the listeners are drawn into it, and hear their own stories as they listen to it. When that happens, their own stories merge with that of the Gospel, and are illuminated by it.

Basically what I've tried to do in this book is to provide a text that speaks clearly. To this end I've used simple, direct, everyday language. I've also incorporated into the text whatever background information is needed so that the reader can readily follow what is happening. Where two or more evangelists carry the same account I've harmonised those accounts. I've fleshed out the episodes where I felt this was called for. Occasionally I've altered the context of a story or a saying of Jesus. Sometimes I've attempted to reconstruct conversations of which the Gospel text only gives hints. I have also simplified a number of difficult areas.

I have told it as one continuous story, beginning with the preaching of John the Baptist, and going right through to Pentecost and the beginnings of the Church. In spite of some significant omissions, I believe the essence of the story is here.

The first version of this book was written for the classroom and in it. It was an attempt at making the Gospel more accessible to young people. This revised edition is again aimed chiefly at the young. But I hope that it might also be appreciated by adults.

Flor McCarthy

Preparing the way for the Lord

The desert is not a very friendly place. It is like a frying pan during the day, and a fridge during the night. But if you were looking for peace and quiet, you could hardly find a better place. In every age people who have wanted to be alone with God have gone there. They are called hermits.

Once there was a hermit by the name of John. Ever since he was a little chiseler in short pants, he knew that God had an important mission for him. Just as athletes have to train long and hard if they hope to be successful, so John knew that in order to carry out his mission, he would have to do some serious spiritual training. Therefore, while he was still a teenager, he left home and went to live in the desert.

His mission was to prepare the people for the coming of the Messiah. When the day finally arrived for him to start that mission, he must have been in good shape spiritually, because he launched himself on it like a whirlwind. He went all around the desert area preaching to everyone he met. It was of him the prophet Isaiah was speaking when he said,

A voice crying in the wilderness
prepare a way for the Lord,
straighten out his paths.
Fill in every valley,
level out every mountain and hill,
because God is coming to save his people.

Word got around and people flocked to hear him. Some probably went just out of curiosity. They wanted to see who this guy was and what he looked like. After all those years living in the desert, John must have been an odd-looking character. If you were to judge him by the clothes he wore and the food he ate, you would write him off as a weirdo. For clothes he wore a rough robe made of camel-hair. And for food, he made do with locusts and wild honey.

But most people went out, not so much to see him, as to hear him. He made a great impression on them, because he preached with sincerity and conviction. Very soon the people began to look on him as a prophet. (A prophet is someone who speaks for God). They got very excited about this because no prophet had appeared for a long time.

John's message was simple but challenging:

'God's messenger is coming. Therefore, you must turn away from your sins, and turn back to God.'

'What exactly must we do?' the people asked him.

'Share your possessions with others,' he answered. 'Those who have clothes to spare, should share them with those who have none. Those who have food to spare, should share it with those who have no food.'

'What should we do?' some tax collectors asked.

'Collect what you are entitled to and no more,' he answered.

'And what should we do?' some soldiers asked.

'Don't rob or use violence against anyone, and be content with your pay,' he said.

After a while he began to baptise those who listened to his message. This is how he got the name John the Baptist. By accepting baptism, people showed that they were willing to change their lives. As time passed John became better known. More and more people came out to him, and were baptised by him in the river Jordan.

One day some Pharisees turned up among the crowd. The Pharisees were very religious people but full of pride. They thought they had no need to change their lives. On seeing them John let fly at them.

'You brood of rattlesnakes!' he said. 'You think you're safe. Don't kid yourselves. Turn away from your sins like everyone else. The axe is laid to the root of the tree. Every tree that does not produce good fruit will be chopped down and burned.'

In spite of this stern warning, the Pharisees ignored John's message.

It's hard to exaggerate what the coming of The Messiah meant to the Jews. However, they had different ideas about him. Many thought, or hoped, that he would be a powerful military leader, who would establish a great kingdom like King David did. False messiahs were constantly appearing, and many people were led astray by them.

Generation after generation had longed to see the coming of the Messiah, but had not seen it. Could John be right? Was the Messiah coming at last? The people naturally got very excited at such a prospect. There was a great air of expectancy abroad. Then some people began to say that John himself was the long-awaited Messiah. But John would have none of this.

'I am not the Messiah,' he told them. 'I'm not even fit to lace his boots. My job is simply to prepare the way for him. I have baptised you with water. He will baptise you with the Holy Spirit and with fire. He will separate the bad from the good, like a farmer at harvest time separates the chaff from the wheat.'

Jesus appears on the scene

MEANWHILE Jesus was living in Nazareth, a little village about seventy miles to the north. He was now thirty years old. What had he been doing all those years? He had been growing up quietly in the shadows. The main influences in his life would have been home, school and synagogue. His teaching shows that he had a deep appreciation of nature, scripture, and the life of the ordinary people. Since his foster father, Joseph, was a carpenter, it is presumed that Jesus too worked as a carpenter.

One day when John looked at the queue of people waiting for baptism, who did he see there but his cousin, Jesus. (Their mothers, Mary and Elizabeth, were first cousins.) He was very surprised. He knew that Jesus didn't belong there. So when his turn came he said to him,

'Hang on, you don't have to be baptised with these.'

But Jesus replied,

'Let it be for the time being.'

'But it isn't right,' John insisted. 'In any case, it's you who should be baptising me, not I baptising you.'

But when Jesus insisted, John agreed to baptise him. Afterwards, as Jesus was coming up out of the river, the sky opened and the Holy Spirit came down on him in the form of a dove. And the Father's voice was heard saying,

'This is my Son with whom I am well pleased.'

John took this as a clear sign from God that Jesus was the one whose appearance he had been waiting for. In other words, he was the Messiah.

Clashing with Satan

THE TIME had come for Jesus to begin the work which God sent him into the world to do. But before beginning it, he decided to spend some time in the desert. He stayed there for forty days, fasting and praying. His only companions were the wild animals. While there he was tempted by the devil.

The devil knew exactly when to launch his attack. After forty days without eating, Jesus was fit to eat a stone. And there were plenty of stones lying around the place, little roundy ones that looked like rock buns.

'Okay,' the devil whispered, 'if you really are God's Son, all you have to do is give the order, and these stones will turn into bread.'

Besides the obvious meaning, the word bread can mean material things in general. It seems that the devil was telling Jesus to use his special powers to give the people all the material things they could possibly want. But Jesus knew that material things by themselves will never satisfy people. His chief task was to nourish their minds and hearts with the word of God. So he answered,

'People don't live on bread alone. They also need the word of God.'

The devil knew he had lost that round, but it didn't stop him from trying again. He now took Jesus off and planted him on the pinnacle of the temple in Jerusalem. Far below them the courtyard was crowded with people. The devil now suggested to Jesus a quick way to catch their attention, and so win a large following for himself. He said, 'If you really are God's Son, throw yourself off. You've nothing to worry about, because the Bible says that God will send angels to catch you before you hit the ground.'

The idea was quite attractive. It was a stunt that would have made him the talk of the city. But Jesus refused to jump. He didn't want screaming fans. He wanted followers, that is, people who would imitate his way of living. So he said,

'The Bible also says you mustn't put God to the test.'

Once again the devil was beaten. But being the crafty old guy that he is, he decided to have one more go. This time he took Jesus to an even higher spot. He took him to the top of a very high mountain. From there he showed him all the kingdoms of the world, saying,

'Do you see all these? I'll give you the whole lot of them, if you'll get down on your knees and worship me. Just think of it – the whole world. Many a king and emperor dreamed of ruling the whole world but never did. You can. All you have to do is worship me. How about it then?'

What he was trying to do was to get Jesus to set up a political kingdom, with all the power and glory that would go with it. Though Jesus had come to set up a kingdom, it was not that kind of kingdom. So he said,

'Get lost, you old devil. The Bible says you must worship God and no one else.'

The devil got the message and left him at once.

Some people find it hard to believe that Jesus could be tempted. But as well as a divine nature, he also had a human nature. Besides, temptation in itself is not a sin. Did the devil actually appear to him? We don't know. The main thing is that his temptations were real, just as ours are, even though Old Nick doesn't appear to us in person.

The experience helped Jesus to clarify in his own mind exactly what his mission was. And once he knew what his mission was, he resolved to make a complete gift of himself to it.

Making friends

FOR SOME time John the Baptist had been telling the people that the long-awaited Messiah was coming soon. One day he was standing on the bank of the river Jordan with two of his disciples, John and Andy. Suddenly he saw Jesus passing by.

'There he goes!' he said. 'He's the one I was telling you about – the man who is to take over from me.'

'You mean the Messiah?' they asked him.

'Yes, he's the lamb of God who will take away the sins of the world.'

Leaving John standing there on his own, the two set off after Jesus. Noticing that he was being followed, Jesus stopped and asked,

'What do you want?'

'We just want to know where you live,' the two answered.

'Come and see,' said Jesus.

It was four o'clock in the afternoon. They went with him, probably to a tent by the river, and they spent the rest of the day together. We've no idea what they talked about. All we know is that Jesus must have made a big impression on them, because early next morning Andy went off looking for his brother, Simon. When he found him he said,

'We've found the Messiah!'

Simon asked no questions but set off at once to meet Jesus. When he reached the place where Jesus was staying, Jesus took one look at him and said,

'So they call you Simon. Well, I'm going to call you Peter.'

Simon didn't object. The word 'Peter' meant rock. He probably fancied himself as a bit of a hard man, and figured that the name suited him. Only later would he understand the reason Jesus gave him that name.

The following day Jesus met Philip and said,

'Follow me.'

Straightaway Philip ran off to find his friend, Nat.

'Nat,' he said, 'we've found the Messiah – the man Moses and all the prophets spoke about.'

'Who is he?' asked Nat.

'He's Jesus.'

'Where does he come from?'

'From Nazareth,' Philip answered.

'The Messiah from Nazareth? You must be kidding! Nothing good ever came from Nazareth!'

'Well, if you won't believe me, why don't you come along and meet the man for yourself.'

Nat agreed to go along. Now Nat was a really straight guy. There was no cunning or guile of any kind in him. When Jesus saw him approaching he said,

'Here comes a genuine guy.'

Thus, right from the start, Jesus showed the gift he had of being able to look into the hearts of people. Completely taken aback on hearing this, Nat said,

'I never laid eyes on you before. How then do you know about me?'

'You were sitting under a fig tree when Philip called you. Isn't that so?' Jesus said.

'Yes,' said Nat, more puzzled than ever. Then he said,

'I believe the others now. I believe that you are the Messiah.'

'Nat, do you mean to tell me that you believe in me simply because I told you that I saw you sitting under the fig tree? I assure you, if you stay with me, you will see and hear far greater things than that.'

Great events often begin very simply. So it was with the work of Jesus. It began through personal contact, and was passed on by word of mouth.

This little group of five – John, Andy, Peter, Philip and Nat – were to form the nucleus of the group that later became known as the Twelve Apostles. We'll meet the others a little later.

Showing his power

Three days later Jesus' mother, Mary, was invited to a wedding at Cana in Galilee. Jesus was also invited and so were his new friends. Everybody knows that a lot of drinking goes on at weddings. Well, at this particular wedding, it seems they went a bit too far. They drank the house dry. Not a drop of wine was left, and plenty of drinking time still to go – in those days wedding celebrations went on for several days. The people were getting restless and the young couple began to blush with embarrassment.

Mary noticed what was happening, and decided to do something about it. No, she didn't go along to the drinkers and ask them if they had any homes to go to. Instead she went to Jesus. Taking him quietly to one side, she said to him,

'Son, they've run out of wine.'

'Mother, this has nothing to do with me,' he replied. 'My hour hasn't come yet.'

Knowing that he wouldn't refuse her anything, she called the servants and said to them,

'Do whatever he tells you.'

Now there were six great big water jars standing there. Each of them could hold between twenty and thirty gallons. Then Jesus said to the servants,

'Fill the jars with water.'

They did as he said, filling the jars up to the brim. Then he said to them,

'Now take a glass of this water and give it to the best man.'

Seemed a crazy thing to do, but they did it. However, by the time they reached the best man, the water had turned into wine, excellent wine at that. When the best man tasted it, he turned to the bridegroom and said,

'Hey, this is really good wine – the best I've tasted all day. Most people serve the good wine first, and the inferior stuff later. By that time the people are half tipsy and can't tell the difference. How come you kept the good wine until now?'

The bridegroom hadn't a clue where the wine had come from. But he wasn't complaining because it saved his day, and didn't cost him a penny.

The first miracle Jesus performed was to change water into wine. Wine is a symbol of joy. In this miracle he showed the kind of powers he had, and the kind of person he was. And his disciples believed in him.

Beginning to preach

Immediately after this Jesus left Nazareth and went to Capernaum. This was a much bigger place than Nazareth. It was situated on the shores of the sea of Galilee, and was an important trading town and fishing port. By the way, the sea of Galilee isn't a sea at all, but an inland lake. Anyhow, it was in Capernaum that Jesus began his preaching. The kernel of his message was,

'God's great day has dawned. His Kingdom has come. Repent, and believe the good news.'

People sat up and began to listen. Here was someone talking, not about bad news, but about good news. Indeed something tremendous was happening. The words of the great prophet Isaiah were being fulfilled:

The people who lived in darkness
have seen a great light
on those who lived in the shadow of death
a light has dawned.

Jesus brought light into the world. His teaching showed people how to live. His compassion showed sinners the way back to God. His mere presence brought peace to anguished souls. The only people who would not benefit from his ministry were those who preferred darkness to light.

Some fishermen get hooked

ONE DAY Jesus was standing on the shore of the lake. There were so many people milling around that he was in danger of getting crushed. Everybody wanted to hear what he had to say. It was then that he noticed two boats moored nearby. One of the boats belonged to Peter who was mending his nets.

'Peter, do you mind if I use your boat?' Jesus said.

'Not at all,' Peter answered.

The two of them got into the boat, drew out a little from the shore, and Jesus taught the people from there. When he had finished he said to Peter,

'Row out into deep water and let down the net for a catch.'

'Master,' Peter replied, 'we fished all night long and caught nothing. What chance then have we of catching anything in broad daylight?' He paused, then added, 'Still, if you say so, I will let down the net.'

He rowed out in front of all those people. When he started to let down the net, some of them probably thought he was mad. But to his own surprise, and to the surprise of everyone else, he made a huge catch of fish. It was so large that he had to call to his friends, James and John, to bring out the second boat. They filled both boats until they were almost sinking.

When they got back to shore, Peter threw himself down at the feet of Jesus and said,

'Master, leave me. I'm a sinful man.'

The fact was that he and his companions were stunned by the huge catch of fish they had made. But Jesus said,

'Do not be afraid, Peter. Follow me, and instead of catching fish, you'll be catching people for God.'

Peter and his companions immediately left everything – the fish, the nets, the boats – and followed Jesus. From that day on you could say they were hooked.

Jesus knew well that Peter was a sinner, but he also knew that he was capable of greatness. So he threw down a challenge to him. We all need someone who accepts us for what we are, but who believes that we are capable of more, and who challenges us to realise it.

A devil in the house of God

ON THE sabbath day Jesus went into the synagogue and gave a sermon there. He was an immediate hit with the ordinary people. As soon as he began to speak they said,

'Here is a man who speaks with his own voice. He is not like our own teachers. All they do is repeat what somebody else has said.'

However, right in the middle of the sermon he was rudely interrupted. In the congregation there was a fellow who was possessed by an evil spirit. Suddenly the man decided to grab a bit of the limelight for himself. He jumped up and screamed at Jesus,

'Go back to Nazareth! Leave us alone! What do you want to do – destroy us? I know who you really are. You are God's Holy One.'

But Jesus sorted him out pretty quickly.

'Shut your mouth!' he ordered.

He was talking to the evil spirit, not to the man. Then he said,

'Now, come out of him!'

The spirit began to throw the poor man around the place. But he soon realised that in Jesus he had met his match. So, with one last frightening and hateful scream, he came out of him. The man was badly shaken but recovered.

The people were astonished by what Jesus had done. They said to one another,

'Here is someone who has something new to say, and who speaks with authority. Even the unclean spirits obey him.'

As a result of this incident Jesus' reputation spread all over Galilee.

No rest for the good

When the service in the synagogue was over, Jesus went to Peter's house for something to eat. Now Peter's mother-in-law was in bed with a fever. They told him about her. He insisted on seeing her immediately, so they took him to her bedside. There he took her hand, and helped her to sit up. Suddenly the fever left her. In fact, she felt so good that she got up and prepared a meal for them.

Now all this was happening on the sabbath day, a day of absolute rest from work. Well, that rest officially came to an end at six o'clock in the evening. That evening on the stroke of six the people began to bring along all those who were sick in mind or body. In no time the house was crowded.

No doubt there was a lot of pushing and shoving as people scrambled to get near Jesus. But he didn't mind. He went around to each of those sick people and cured them. His words healed the spirit, and his touch healed the body. It must have been all hours by the time he got to bed. Nevertheless, he was up at the crack of dawn next morning. In fact, it was still dark as he slipped out of the house, and went off to a lonely place to pray.

Jesus prayed not only out of a sense of duty but also out of a sense of need. Like all those who spend themselves working for others, Jesus faced the danger of burn-out. He needed to recharge his batteries. One of the ways he did this was through prayer.

However, that particular morning he didn't get much time to himself. Very soon he was missed, and Peter and his friends went looking for him. When they found him they said,

'Everybody is looking for you.'

He didn't tell them to get lost and leave him alone. He just said,

'Let's move on to the next town. I must preach the good news there also.'

He visited the synagogues all around Galilee. Sick and desperate people of every kind came to him, or were brought to him, and at his word and at his touch were restored to health. Huge crowds flocked to him. People came from as far away as Jerusalem, and even from beyond the Jordan. And it wasn't only Jews that came. Non-Jews (Gentiles) came too. He made no distinction between them, but treated them all with the same kindness.

Chatting at a well

Once on returning from a visit to Judea Jesus took a shortcut through Samaria. We must remember that he was a Jew. Now the Jews regarded the Samaritans as pagans. As a matter of fact, the Jews and the Samaritans hadn't been on friendly terms for about four hundred years. If that sounds crazy, all you have to do is think of Northern Ireland, where the roots of the present troubles go back three hundred years.

Jesus and his friends stopped at a well about half a mile outside the village of Sychar. It was midday and the sun was at its hottest. Jesus was tired so he sat down beside the well. He was also very thirsty. But, without a bucket, there was no way he could get a drink because the well was too deep. Meanwhile his friends had gone into the village to buy food.

Then a Samaritan woman arrived with a bucket to draw water. It seems that she was an outcast in the village because of the kind of life she was living. Jesus said to her,

'Give me a drink.'

The woman was amazed that a Jewish man would speak to her, let alone ask her for a favour. When she recovered from the shock, she said,

'You must be the first Jewish man in history to ask a Samaritan woman for a drink.'

She gave him the bucket of water. He sank his head in it and took a long drink. Then he said,

'Thank you. You're very generous. But if only you knew how generous God is, and who I am, then it is you who would have asked me for a drink. And I wouldn't have given you this stagnant water. I would have given you running water.'

She was beginning to like this stranger. She was lost and mixed up. Most people either avoided her or pointed the finger at her. But here was someone who was friendly and treated her with respect. It encouraged her to continue the chat. She said,

'The well is very deep, and you have no bucket. How then can you give me water?'

'Actually, I wasn't talking about this kind of water,' he answered gently. 'You know well that those who drink this water will get thirsty again. But those who drink the water I can give, will never know thirst again. It will be as if they had an eternal spring inside them.'

Jesus, of course, was not talking about ordinary water. Nor was he talking about ordinary thirst. He was talking about the thirst in the human heart which only God can quench. Even though the woman hadn't a clue what he was on about she said,

'Any chance I could have some of the water you're talking about, so that I won't have to come here every day to draw this well-water?'

'Sure,' said Jesus, 'but first I want you to go home and come back here with your husband.'

'I've no husband,' she answered.

'That's right. You've had five husbands. That means the man you are living with now is not really your husband.'

So he knew about her! Right from the start she felt that he was looking into her heart. And yet he didn't make her feel bad – only just a little uncomfortable. Still, she thought it better to change the subject.

'Sir,' she said, 'I can see that you are a prophet. Well then, maybe you can put me right about something. We Samaritans have always worshipped God here on Mount Gerizim (a mountain in Samaria). But you Jews claim that the only place to worship God is in Jerusalem. Who's right?'

'It's not the place you worship God in that matters, but the spirit you show,' Jesus replied. 'My dear woman, the time is coming, in fact it is already here, when people will be able to worship God anywhere they choose, provided they do so with a sincere heart.'

'It's all a mystery to me,' she replied. 'All I know is that when the Messiah comes, he'll explain everything to us.'

Then Jesus came right out and said,
'I am the Messiah.'

Before she could take in this astounding truth, the disciples arrived back with the grub. They were very surprised to see Jesus talking to a Samaritan woman. But as soon as she saw them coming, she took to her heels. She ran all the way back into the village. She was so excited that she forgot the bucket and the water.

Jesus' friends opened up the grub and said,
'Master, have something to eat. You must be starving.'

But he said,
'No, I'm not. You see, I have a secret food that keeps me going.'

This puzzled them so they asked,
'What food are you talking about, and who gave it to you?'

Jesus wasn't talking about ordinary food. He said,
'My food is to do the will of my Father. When he sent me into the world, he gave me a job to do. To do that job is what I live for. That is the food that keeps me going.'

Meanwhile, the woman had reached the village. To everyone she met she said,
'Come out and meet a man who told me the whole story of my life. He says he's the Messiah.'

Many went out to see Jesus. They were so impressed that they invited him into the village. He accepted their invitation and stayed two days there. As a result many of them believed in him. When he had gone they said to the woman,
'We believe that he is the saviour of the world, not because you told us, but because we've met him ourselves.'

The woman was greatly enriched as a result of her encounter with Jesus. Yet he didn't give her anything. On the contrary, he asked something from her. In so doing he awakened her to her own riches. The greatest good we can do for other people is not to give them of our own wealth, but to show them their own.

The man who came in from the cold

In those days the most feared disease of all was leprosy. There was no cure for it, and it was considered to be highly contagious. For this reason lepers were forced to live outside the community. They were like diseased branches that had been lopped off a tree. They were known as the untouchables.

Theirs was a cold, lonely existence. They had said goodbye to home, family and friends. They had no hope. Their bodies were falling apart. Their life was a living death. People believed they were cursed by God. They considered them to be not only sick but also unclean.

One day Jesus was entering a town when a leper appeared from nowhere. He was a very bad case. The people moved out of the way to avoid him. Of course, he shouldn't have appeared in public without ringing a bell, or shouting the warning, 'Unclean, unclean'. He ran the risk of being chased away with stones. But he was determined to meet the one man he believed would not reject him and who could cure him.

The leper came right up to Jesus, and threw himself on his knees in front of him. Jesus didn't try to avoid him. He stood his ground. Then, seeing the state he was in, he took pity on him, and did something which no doubt shocked the onlookers. He reached out his hand and touched him. By touching the leper Jesus became unclean himself.

We feel honoured when someone important shakes hands with us or gives us a pat on the back. Imagine how good the leper felt when Jesus touched him. He felt he was a human being after all. His body was horribly wounded by leprosy. But his spirit was even more deeply wounded by the sense of having been rejected and abandoned by everyone, including God. By touching him Jesus healed his wounded spirit. Then the leper said,

'Sir, I believe you can cure me if you really want to.'

'Of course I want to,' Jesus replied. 'Stand up. You're cured.'

The man stood up, and immediately the incredible happened. His sores vanished. His skin returned to its natural colour. In short, he was cured. Then Jesus said to him,

'Don't tell anyone about this. Just go to one of the priests, and get yourself a certificate, so that you can prove to everyone that you're cured.'

Instead of keeping his mouth shut as Jesus had told him, the leper told everyone he met what Jesus had done for him. As a result of this publicity, Jesus could no longer enter a village without being recognised. He was forced to stay out in the country. But even there he couldn't find a hiding place, and people flocked to him from every quarter.

The man who was let down by his friends

JESUS WENT back to Capernaum, perhaps hoping to get some rest. No such luck. Word got out that he was staying in a certain house. Immediately people headed for the place, and in no time you had a full house. Jesus was in one of the inner rooms, teaching the people who were packed like sardines. Suddenly these four guys arrived outside with a friend of theirs. He was a cripple, and they were carrying him on a stretcher.

The four men quickly summed up the situation. They realised there was no way they were going to be able to get their friend in through the door with all those people crowding round it. Like most houses in those days, the house had a flat roof. An outside stairs lead on to the roof. This was the answer to their problem. Without a moment's hesitation their leader said,

'Right lads, up on to the roof with him.'

Up they went and set the man down there. Then they took some of the tiles away until they made a large hole. Now came the tricky bit. How to let their friend down safely into the room where Jesus was. The last thing they wanted to do was to drop him, in case he ended up in a worse state.

Meanwhile, down in the room itself, we can imagine the surprise the people got when daylight began to appear above their heads. Then the stretcher appeared, and the four guys letting it down gingerly by means of ropes. Jesus saw what they were up to, but didn't get annoyed about being interrupted. In fact, he was delighted to see how much faith they had in him, and all the trouble they had gone to on behalf of their friend.

Somehow a bit of room was found, and the stretcher with the man aboard arrived in front of Jesus. Jesus looked at the man and saw that he was in need of spiritual healing too. And since he regarded spiritual healing as more important than physical healing, he decided to begin with that. He said to him,

'Friend, your sins are forgiven.'

Now, in the audience were some of the religious leaders. These were shocked when they heard Jesus say, 'Your sins are forgiven.' They started to mutter to one another,

'Just who does he think he is? Only God can forgive sins.'

But Jesus knew what they were thinking, so he said,

'Okay, I can see that you don't believe that I have the power to forgive sins. Well then, I'll show you that I have. To prove it, I'm going to cure this man.'

Then, turning to the crippled man, he said,

'I want you to get up, fold up your stretcher, and go home.'

The man stood up immediately. Not a trace of the wobbles. Then he folded up his stretcher and headed for the door. The people drew aside and he squeezed past. They were absolutely astonished, and praised God saying,

'We've never seen anything like this before.'

The man went off home feeling at least ten feet tall. His soul was bright and clean and at peace. And underneath him he had a pair of legs that could do what legs were meant to do.

A tax collector joins

Afterwards Jesus left the house and went down to the shore. He probably needed some fresh air because it must have been very stuffy in that crowded house. But once again the people gathered round him, so he continued to teach them right there on the beach.

When he finally got away from them he passed by the Tax Office. Sitting on the steps in front of the building was a tax collector by the name of Matthew. Jesus looked at him. He didn't utter any threats or offer any rewards. He just said,

'Matt, follow me.'

And guess what? Matthew got up at once, left everything, and followed him.

Collecting taxes was not a popular occupation. It may be that Matthew was finding the job soul-destroying. So when Jesus offered him the chance to do something better with his life, he grabbed it immediately and with both hands. And yet it can't have been easy for him. Tax-collecting was a secure and lucrative job.

As a tax collector Matthew would have learned to keep accurate accounts. Later on he put what he had learned to good use. He wrote down an account of many of the things Jesus did and said. We owe one of the Gospels to him.

Birds of a feather

That evening Matthew threw a party for Jesus in his house. Naturally, he invited along his old buddies. So, sitting at table, Jesus found himself surrounded by tax collectors and sinners. Indeed, many of these had become followers of his.

Jesus didn't just tolerate sinners. He welcomed them. He provided the kind of presence in which they felt accepted and loved as they were. In this atmosphere they were able to respond and change.

The religious leaders, on the other hand, despised sinners. Consequently they were shocked to see Jesus eating and drinking with them. But they didn't have the courage to tell him this to his face. Instead they went and complained to the apostles.

'Why does your master eat with tax collectors and sinners?' they asked.

But Jesus had heard what they said, and asked them a question:

'Who does a doctor work for? For healthy people or for sick people?'

'For sick people,' they answered.

'Well, now you know why I mix with these people. They are sick, sick spiritually, and are not ashamed to admit it. But they want to get well. It was precisely to help people like them to get well that I came.'

Watching like hawks

In the Synagogue

One sabbath day Jesus went into a synagogue. Right in front of him he saw a man with a withered hand. The man had probably been placed there deliberately to see if Jesus would cure him on the sabbath day. If he did, then the religious leaders could bring a very serious charge against him – that of breaking the sabbath.

The sabbath was very important to the Jews, and they observed it scrupulously. There were some thirty-nine different categories of work which were prohibited on that day. For instance, you couldn't light a fire, prepare food, visit the sick, walk more than about half a mile, or heal a person.

Hence, as soon as Jesus entered that synagogue, the religious leaders were watching like hawks to see if he would heal the man with the withered hand. But Jesus knew what their game was, and decided to take them on. He turned his attention first to the man with the withered hand. He said,

'Step out into the middle.'

The man did so willingly. All he wanted was a cure, sabbath or no sabbath. With one useless hand he really was only half a man.

Then, turning to the religious leaders, Jesus said,

'Tell me something. Is it permitted to cure a person on the sabbath?'

But they refused to answer.

'Okay,' said he, 'so you won't answer me. Well then, let me ask you another question. Suppose one of you has a sheep, and it falls into a hole on the sabbath day, would you pull it out?'

Still no reply. Only sour looks. So he answered the question himself.

'Of course you would. Many of you, I'm sure, have often done so. And never for a moment did you think you were breaking the sabbath. Now if it's okay to save a sheep on the sabbath, surely it's okay to save a human being?'

Then he turned back to the man and said,

'Stretch out your hand.'

The man did so and his hand came right. And Jesus said to them all,

'Learn a lesson from this. The sabbath was made for people, not people for the sabbath.'

The ordinary people were delighted at the way things had turned out, but the Pharisees were raging. They were so angry that they began to plot how to kill Jesus.

At a dinner

Another sabbath day Jesus was invited to dinner by a leading Pharisee. But again it was a set-up, because they had planted a sick man there to see if he would cure him on the sabbath. Jesus took the initiative by asking them the same question he had asked on the previous occasion,

'Is it right to cure a man on the sabbath?'

But they wouldn't answer. He then took the sick man by the hand, cured him in front of them all, and sent him away.

Then he turned to the leaders and said,

'Is there any one of you, if his son fell into a well on the sabbath day, would leave him to drown? Of course not. You'd pull him out at once. In fact, you'd do as much for one of your animals. So then, is it wrong for me to cure a man on the sabbath?'

Still no answer – only silence. On seeing this he continued,

'The very moment I entered this house I knew you were watching me. Well, I have been watching you too, and I have noticed certain things about you. I noticed, for instance, how you tried to grab the places of honour at the top table.

'If you are invited to a wedding, don't sit at the top table. Somebody more important than you may have been invited. Then the best man will come to you and say, 'That place is reserved. Would you mind sitting at the bottom table.' You'll have to get up in front of all the guests, and go and take a seat at the bottom table. Instead, when you are invited to a wedding, take a seat at the bottom table. Then the best man will come and say to you, 'What are you doing down here? Come on up to the top table.' Then you'll have honour before all the other guests.'

He paused, then continued,

'There's something else that I've noticed.'

Then turning to the man who had invited him, he said,

'I see that all your guests are well-off, respectable people, and all friends of yours. No doubt they will invite you to their homes in return. But I don't see any poor people here, or any crippled people, or blind people. No, of course not, because the likes of them would never be able to throw a party for you.

'In other words, the name of the game is: you scratch my back, and I'll scratch yours. Now if you think you'll get a reward in heaven for this sort of thing, you're codding yourself. You're getting your reward here on earth, and believe me, that's the only reward you'll get.

'If you want to do something worthy of the Kingdom of Heaven, invite in poor people, who will never be able to return the compliment. Then your generosity will be genuine, and you will get a rich reward in heaven.'

A night-time visitor

One night Jesus had a very surprising visitor. His name was Nicodemus. Nicodemus was not only a teacher and leader, but also a Pharisee.

The Pharisees took their religion very seriously. They were not priests but lay people. For them religion meant keeping God's Commandments – nothing wrong with that. However, besides the Ten Commandments, which God gave them through Moses, they had a whole lot of other rules, which they claimed also came down from Moses. These were called the Traditions.

Jesus saw that many of these rules were more of a hindrance than a help. So he had no hesitation in setting them aside, and in teaching his followers to do the same. That was why the Pharisees were so hostile to him. He had numerous clashes with them, as we will see.

Another bunch of people Jesus clashed with were the Scribes. It was the job of the Scribes to interpret the above rules.

Nicodemus had come to see Jesus because he had heard about the great things he was doing. He came by night, probably because he didn't want to be seen by the others. Still, there can be no doubt but that he was a sincere man. They had a long conversation. It's obvious that Nicodemus was impressed. He turns up twice later in the story, and each time as a friend of Jesus.

Picking his team

WE HAVE seen how, right from the beginning, Jesus had crowds of people around him everywhere he went. No doubt some of them were there for what they could get out of him, and others were there out of curiosity. But there were many who took his message seriously and who wanted to follow him. These are called *disciples*.

Jesus now decided that the time had come to pick a small band of people who would always be with him, and who would help him with his work. Before picking them he went off into the hills to pray about it. Early next morning he came back and announced his team. We've met some of them already. Anyway, here it is:

SIMON: Jesus changed his name to Peter, which means rock. At times Peter was as solid as a rock. But at other times he was more like a piece of jelly.

ANDREW: He was Peter's brother and, like him, was a fisherman.

JAMES and JOHN: These were brothers, also fishermen. They were hot-tempered and earned themselves a nickname – The Sons of Thunder. Believe it or not, it was Jesus who gave them this nickname.

PHILIP and BARTHOLOMEW: These seem to have been pals. We don't know what they did to earn a crust of bread. Bartholomew is believed to be the same person as NAT, whom we met earlier.

MATTHEW: There were a lot of raised eyebrows when his name was called out. He was a tax collector and they were hated. They're not exactly popular today either.

THOMAS: He too earned himself a nickname. He came to be known as the Doubter. We'll see why later.

JAMES: He was the son of Alphaeus. We don't know much about him except that he is usually called James the Lesser, to distinguish him from the chap above, who is called James the Greater.

SIMON: He was another very surprising choice. He belonged to a band of people called the Zealots. These had one aim – to get the Romans out of Palestine. Today they would probably be called terrorists.

JUDE: He was the son of another James. He is the patron saint of hopeless cases. Not a bad chap to be friendly with!

JUDAS ISCARIOT: Everybody knows his name and what he did. It's not surprising that every time the apostles are listed, his name is always put last.

So there you have them. The apostles were just twelve ordinary people. But Jesus saw good in each one of them, even in Judas.

Sermon on a hill

When preachers are giving a sermon, they go up into a pulpit so that everybody in church can see and hear them. On one occasion there were so many people gathered to hear Jesus, that he had to go up on to a hill to speak to them.

The first thing he did was to get everybody to sit down. Not a bad idea because the sermon went on a bit long. But it was very important and contained the heart of his teaching. It starts off with the eight Beatitudes. These are eight paths to happiness. They can also be seen as eight qualities which Jesus wanted to see in his followers.

The eight Beatitudes

'Happy are the poor in spirit, the Kingdom of Heaven is theirs.'

(Most people think that you have to be rich to be happy. But wise people know that this is not so. As human beings we are always poor and weak. Our hopes are very fragile, and can collapse in a minute. We need God. Happy those who put their trust in God rather than in money. Money will let you down, but God will never let you down.)

'Happy are the gentle, they will inherit the earth.'

(Most people think that it is the guys who throw their weight around, the bullies, who always get what they want. But who likes a bully? No one. So how can a bully be happy? But everybody loves a gentle person. The gentle person will never be short of friends. Having friends makes you happy.)

'Happy are those who mourn, they will be comforted.'

(Most people would say that the happy ones are the ones who live it up, without a thought for God or man. It's not so. To be happy one has to be a caring person. This caring will sometimes break your heart. Don't be afraid to show your hurt, even your tears. They are precious to God. He will dry them.)

'Happy are those who hunger and thirst for what is right, they will get their fill.'

(To live rightly is what life is about. Those who knowingly do wrong can't be happy. They will feel wrong inside. Make it your first aim, then, to live a good life. Put it even before eating and drinking. Then you will begin to taste real happiness.)

'Happy are those who show mercy, they will get mercy in return.'

(Some people get their kicks out of hurting others. It makes them feel important. But does it make them happy? It's very doubtful. They live in fear that some day someone will give them a taste of their own medicine. But those who show kindness and forgiveness to others are happy people. They feel good inside themselves. And God will treat them in the same kind way they treated others. Then their happiness will be complete.)

'Happy are the clean of heart, they will see God.'

(Many people take great care to see that their fingernails and skin are clean. That's okay, but it's still only outer cleanness. The cleanness that really matters is inner cleanness – cleanness of mind and heart. If you are clean and bright inside yourself, you will be able to see the world in the same way. That is a giant step on the road to happiness.)

'Happy are the peacemakers, they will be called the children of God.'

(Some people get a high out of causing trouble. They seem to be born trouble-makers – as if Old Nick was their father. But, once again, ask yourself: Are trouble-makers happy people? Of course not. How could they be? Are they not all turmoil and unrest inside themselves? But how different the peacemaker is. Peacemakers are at peace with themselves. And what a lovely feeling that is! They try to share that peace with others. In this way they are behaving like true children of God.)

'Happy are those who suffer for what is right, the Kingdom of Heaven is theirs.'

(To do the right thing is not always easy. Sometimes it will make you unpopular. You will have to suffer. Still, it's a great feeling to be trying to live the way God wants you to live. Even if outside you things are rough and the rain is falling, inside you the sun is shining. You know that God is pleased with you. No one can rob you of that feeling. It is a foretaste of heaven.)

Salt and light

You are the salt of the earth. Just as salt adds flavour to food and keeps it from going bad, so you are to add the flavour of goodness to life and keep it healthy by your high standards.

You are the light of the world. No one lights a lamp and puts it under a tub. They put it on a lamp-stand so that it can give light to all in the house. Let the light of your goodness shine for all to see. On seeing your good deeds, people will give praise to God.

Old ways must go

Don't model yourselves on the Scribes and Pharisees. Unless your goodness goes deeper than theirs, you will never enter the Kingdom of Heaven. What I'm saying is – the old ways and the old teachings are no longer good enough. Things must change.

For instance, in the old days you were told: Thou shalt not kill. I want you to do a lot better than that. You can hurt people in a whole lot of ways without killing them. I'm saying to you that you must not hurt others at all.

Suppose you are in church, in the very act of offering a gift to God, and suddenly you remember that somebody has something against you, what should you do? Most people would say: go right ahead with what you're doing, because the worship of God comes first. But I say no. I say you must leave your gift there, and go and make it up with the person concerned. Then, and only then, should you come back and offer your gift to God.

There was another rule in the old days which said: An eye for an eye, and a tooth for a tooth. In other words – give as good as you get. But I say to you: if someone treats you badly, do not retaliate. Two wrongs never made a right.

Again, in the old days you were told: Love your friends, and hate your enemies. But I say to you: love your enemies. Pray for those who make life difficult for you. If you do this, you will show that you are true children of God.

Look at the way God treats people. He lets the sun shine on bad people as well as good people. And he lets the rain fall on the field of the crook as well as the field of the honest man.

If you love only your friends, that's no big deal. Even gangsters love their own. And if you salute only your own cronies, there's nothing exceptional about that. If you want to be different – do as God does. Treat everybody the same.

The golden rule

You don't like other people to judge you harshly, right? Well then, don't you judge them harshly.

You don't like other people to condemn you. Well then, don't you condemn them either.

You like others to forgive you. Well, they like you to forgive them too. So forgive them.

You like others to be generous with you. Well, they like you to be generous with them. So be generous with them.

Here is the golden rule which sums it all up: *Treat others the way you would like them to treat you.*

Correcting others

Lots of people want to put the world right, but they go the wrong way about it. They begin with others instead of themselves.

How is it that you can see a speck of sawdust in another person's eye, and if there was a plank of wood in your own eye you couldn't see it?

Tell me something. Can one blind person lead another? Of course not, unless they both want to end up in the ditch.

What I'm saying is: put your own house in order first. Then maybe you can help others to put their house in order.

Don't be a show-off

Be careful not to parade your good deeds before other people. Don't go around blowing your own trumpet to let everybody know what a great person you are. Because if you do, then don't expect to get a reward in heaven from God. You will already have got your reward here on earth, namely, the praise of people.

Instead, do your good deeds quietly. Don't let your left hand know what your right hand is doing. God sees everything that is going on, even what is done in secret. He will reward you.

Treasure hunting

Don't pile up treasures for yourselves here on earth. Earthly goods don't last. If the thieves don't rob them on you, rust or moths or woodworm or something else will eventually destroy them.

The right place to lay up treasure is in heaven. There are no robbers there – at least no active ones. You won't find any rust or moths or woodworm there either. So your treasure will be absolutely safe.

If your treasure is here on earth, your heart will be here too. But if your treasure is in heaven, your heart will be in heaven too.

No one can serve two masters. You don't need brains to see that. Neither can you serve God and money.

Quit worrying

Don't worry about things like food and drink and clothes. There are more important things in life.

Why get all worked up about food? Look at the birds of the air. They don't plant anything or reap anything. Yet they don't starve. Who feeds them? God does.

Now if God cares for them, he will care for you too. You mean a lot more to him than they do.

And why get all hot and bothered about clothes? Look at the wild flowers. See how beautiful they are! Not even King Solomon had a robe that could match them for beauty. And all this beauty doesn't cost them one drop of sweat. God gives it to them for nothing.

Now if God takes such good care of them, then you can be sure that he will take care of you too.

So stop worrying about material things. Let people who have no belief in God or in an after-life worry about them.

Put spiritual things first. Make it your first concern to seek the Kingdom of God and to live good lives. If you do that, then everything else will fall into place.

The two roads

There are two roads you can follow in life.

The first is broad and easy to travel. All you have to do is follow the crowd. It is downhill all the way. It is the way of comfort and ease. Many people are fooled and travel down this road. But in the long run it gets them nowhere. In fact it leads to ruin.

The second road is narrow and difficult. You will often have to go it alone. It is uphill most of the way. It is the way of self-sacrifice and struggle. Few take this road. But they are the lucky ones, because this road leads to life.

Don't be led astray

People will try to lead you astray. Therefore, be on the look out for false prophets – people who claim to speak for God but who are con-artists. Don't be taken in by them. On the outside they may look like sheep, but underneath they are hungry wolves.

How will you be able to recognise them? Like this. A healthy tree produces good fruit. A diseased tree produces bad fruit. Therefore, to tell a healthy tree from a diseased tree, all you have to do is look at the fruit.

If you want to tell a true prophet from a false one, all you have to do is look at the fruit they produce with their lives. By fruit I mean their deeds. If people's deeds are good, it means they are good. If their deeds are evil, it means they are evil. It's as simple as that.

Words are not enough

It is not those who say, 'Lord, I love you', who will enter the Kingdom of Heaven, but those who do the will of God in their lives. What I mean is: words alone will not get you into heaven. You must have deeds to back them up.

I've said many things to you in the course of this sermon. Some of you will benefit from what I've said, others won't.

Those who listen to my teaching and who put it into practice, are like the wise people who built their house on a rock. Rain beat down on it, floods hurled themselves against it, gales lashed it, but it stood firm. Why? Because it was built on a rock.

But those who listen to my teaching and who let it in one ear and out the other, are like the fools who built their house on sand. Rain beat down on it, floods hurled themselves against it, gales lashed it, and it collapsed. Why? Because it was built on sand.

If you build your lives on my words, you are building them on solid rock. Heaven and earth will pass away, but my words will never pass away.

The people were enthralled, not only by what Jesus said, but by the way he said it. He spoke like one who knew what he was talking about.

A soldier's faith

Not long after this Jesus entered Capernaum once more. A centurion (an officer in the Roman army) got wind of his coming. He had a problem – one of his servants was sick. In fact, the servant was dying. When the centurion heard that Jesus was coming to town, he sent a couple of his Jewish friends to meet him and put in a good word for him. These came to Jesus and put the man's case very well. They said,

'If anyone deserves a break, he does. He's a good man and a friend of the Jewish people. He built a synagogue for us.'

On hearing this Jesus decided to go at once to the centurion's house. But before he got there, the centurion sent messengers to tell him,

'Sir, don't put yourself to all this trouble just for my sake. I don't deserve to have you under my roof. In any case, you don't have to come to me. All you have to do is give the order, and my servant will get well.

'As an army officer I know all about giving orders. I say to one of my soldiers "Go!" and he goes, or "Come here!" and he comes. To my servants all I have to say is "Do this!" and they do it. You can do the same. Just say the word, and my servant will be cured.'

Jesus was flabbergasted at the man's faith. He said so to those who were with him at the time,

'Did you hear that? This man is a foreigner. Yet he has greater faith than you, who call yourselves God's own people. The trouble with you is that you think you have it made. You think you are the only ones who will be saved. Well, I've got news for you. People will come from the east and from the west, from the north and from the south – foreigners of all shapes and sizes – and they will sit down at the feast of God's kingdom, while some of you will find yourselves locked out.'

This can't have gone down well with his listeners. In fact, it would have hurt and angered them. But sometimes one has to be cruel to be kind. In any case, it was meant as a warning.

Then Jesus said to the messengers,

'Go back and tell the man that his servant will live.'

When they got back home it was exactly as Jesus had said. The man's servant was alive and well.

Stopped on the way to the graveyard

About this time Jesus went to a town called Nain. His friends were with him as usual, and a whole lot of other people as well. Just as they were approaching the gate of the town, they saw a large crowd coming towards them. When they heard the music of flutes and a lot of crying and wailing, they knew that it was a funeral. They stepped aside to let it pass.

They didn't use coffins in those days. The body was carried to the place of burial on a kind of stretcher. Judging from the number of people who had shown up, they presumed that it was some big shot who had died. But they soon discovered that it was a little shot. In fact, it was a young boy who was being buried. It was a very sad case. The mother was a widow, and the little fellow was her only son.

Naturally the poor woman was in a terrible state. It was heart-breaking to look at her. She and all those around her were in tears. Jesus was deeply moved when he saw what was happening. His heart went out to that mother. Just as she was passing by, supported by her friends, he went over to her and said gently,

'Stop crying.'

Then he went up and put his hand on the stretcher. With that, the men who were carrying it stood still. By now all eyes were riveted on Jesus. Then, looking directly at the dead boy, he said,

'Young man, I order you to get up.'

And the young lad sat up at once and began to talk. He must have got a heck of a fright when he discovered where they were taking him. We can imagine him saying something like,

'Hey! What are you doing to me? Where are you taking me? To the graveyard? No, thank you!'

He jumped off that stretcher like a light. Then Jesus took him by the hand and led him to his mother. After she gave him a few good hugs he felt okay – as if the whole thing had been nothing more than a bad dream. As for the mother, her tears continued to fall, only now they were tears of joy.

The people were shaken by what they had witnessed, and it was no wonder. But when they recovered from the shock, they knew for sure that the hand of God was in it. So they began to praise God saying,

'A great prophet has come among us. God has once again visited his people.'

News of what Jesus had done spread like wildfire through the whole of Judaea and the surrounding countryside.

Gate-crashing the party

A PHARISEE by the name of Simon invited Jesus to his house for a meal. Jesus accepted the invitation, but when he got there, Simon didn't treat him very nicely.

It was the custom at that time to do three things for an honoured guest. As soon as he arrived, you gave him the kiss of peace as a sign of welcome. Then you gave him a basin of water to wash his dusty feet. Finally, you poured a little perfume on his head. These were just normal signs of courtesy. Yet, for some reason, Simon didn't give any of them to Jesus. So Jesus sat down to the meal just as he was.

They didn't use chairs in those days. They lay down on couches, resting on the left elbow, leaving the right hand free to reach for the grub. The feet were stretched out behind, and the sandals were taken off during the meal. Now you've got a picture of the scene.

Jesus rarely got a chance to sit down and relax like anybody else. Usually something unexpected happened. This time was no exception. Just as he lay back and started to tuck into the grub, who should gate-crash the party but a woman who had a very bad name in the town. On seeing her Simon got red with embarrassment.

The woman came up behind Jesus and knelt down at his feet. Suddenly the rottenness of her life hit her. Down came her tears in a flood, right on top of Jesus' tired and dusty feet. She looked around for a towel, but no one gave her one. So what did she do? She dried his feet with her hair. Then she kissed them, and poured perfume on them.

Meanwhile old Simon was watching all this and was thinking,

'If this man was a holy man, he would know the kind of woman she is, and wouldn't allow her to touch him.'

But Jesus said to him,

'Simon, I know what you're thinking. Let me tell you a little story. A certain man had two debtors. The first owed him £5,000, the second £50. Neither of the two could pay him. But he was a kind-hearted man. He wrote off the debt for both of them. Now which of them will love him the more?'

'The one who owed him £5,000,' answered Simon.

'Correct,' said Jesus. Then pointing to the woman he said,

'Now consider this woman. When I entered your house this evening, you gave me no water to wash my feet. But she washed them with her tears and dried them with her hair. You gave me no kiss of peace either. But she got down on her knees and kissed my very feet. Neither did you think it worth your while to put some perfume on my head. But she not only put perfume on my head but on my feet as well. Her many sins are forgiven her. That is why she has shown such great love.'

Then turning to the woman, he said,

'Your sins are forgiven.'

When the people who were sitting at table with him heard him say this they began to mutter,

'Who is he, that he even forgives sins?'

But Jesus ignored what they were saying and spoke to the woman again, saying,

'It was your faith that saved you. Now go in peace.'

Jesus saw that there was another and better side to the woman. By graciously accepting her service, he helped her to believe in that side and to let it unfold.

After her encounter with Jesus, she was walking again with the moon and the stars.

A day of story-telling

One day Jesus went down to the shore of the lake. he probably just wanted to relax and get away from it all for a while. But once again the people gathered around him. So he got into a boat, sat down, and began to teach them from there. The people were sitting all along the shore, right down to the water's edge. He taught them about the Kingdom of heaven by means of stories.

The sower

Jesus spent much of his time preaching the word of God to the people. In this story he compares the word of God to a seed.

'The Kingdom of Heaven is like a farmer who went out to sow seed in his field. Some of the seed fell on a path which ran through the field. The soil there was rock-hard, with the result that the seed had no chance of putting down roots. It lay there on the surface. Then the birds came along and said, 'Thank you very much for the picnic,' and gobbled it up.

'Other seed fell on stony ground where the soil was very thin. It sprang up almost immediately. But it didn't last very long. When the weather got hot, it withered away because of lack of soil and moisture.

'More seed fell among weeds. It came up all right, but so too did the weeds. The weeds said, 'Where do you think you're going, you little upstart?" That was the end of the seed. The greedy weeds choked it.

'Finally, some seed fell on good ground. It grew up and produced a harvest. In some cases thirty per cent, in some cases sixty per cent, and in some cases even a hundred per cent.'

He paused to give the people a chance to think about the story. But the apostles didn't get the point of it, so they asked him to explain it to them.

'Okay,' he said. 'I wasn't going to explain it. But I'll make an exception for you since you are my right-hand men. But the others will have to figure it out for themselves. Here is what the story means.

'The seed is the word of God. The minds and hearts of people are the ground in which this seed is planted. The seed that fell on the path, and which was gobbled up by the wild birds, stands for those who hear the word of God but who fail to grasp its meaning. The devil comes along and snatches it away from them. And that's the end of that.

'The seed that fell on stony ground and which withered away, stands for those who hear the word and welcome it with joy. But it doesn't sink into their minds and hearts. So when they have to suffer some trial or persecution because of the word, they quickly throw the towel in, and the message dies within them.

'The seed that fell among the weeds stands for those who hear the word of God and receive it with enthusiasm. But they have so many other things on their mind – cares, worries, problems, greed for money, and so on – that the word gets crowded out, and dies without producing any results.

'Finally, the seed that fell on good soil, well, that should be obvious. It stands for those who hear the word, take it to heart and put it into practice, so that it changes their lives.

'Now have you got the message?' he asked.

'Message received, loud and clear,' they answered.

The wheat and the weeds

'The Kingdom of Heaven is like a man who sowed good seed in his field. He did a very thorough job and went home that evening feeling that he had earned his supper. That night he slept like a log. But while he was asleep, an enemy of his came along and played a really lousy trick on him. He sowed weeds among the wheat. Nobody noticed anything.

'A couple of weeks went by and up came the young blades of wheat. They were fresh and green and lovely. People congratulated the farmer on the success of his sowing, and said that he would surely get a bumper harvest from the field. But then, all of a sudden, the weeds appeared. The farmer's workers were very upset. They couldn't figure out where the weeds had come from. So they went to the farmer and said.

"We know that you sowed good seed in the field. Well then, where did the weeds come from?"

"An enemy is responsible for this," he said.

"That's terrible," they answered. "The weeds will ruin the crop. If you like we'll go out and pull them up."

"I appreciate your concern, but that's not on," the farmer replied. "If you did that you would trample on the young wheat. Besides, in pulling up the weeds, you would be bound to pull up some of the wheat as well."

"What do you want us to do then?" they asked.

"There's really nothing you can do," he said, "We'll just have to let them both grow until the harvest-time. Then we'll separate them. We'll gather up the weeds into bundles and make a bonfire of them. And we'll gather the wheat and store it in the barn."'

The apostles didn't get the point of this story either, so Jesus had to explain it to them.

'The farmer stands for God, and farmer's enemy stands for the devil. The field is the world. Just as the farmer's field contained a mixture of wheat and weeds, so the world contains a mixture of good and evil, of honest people and crooks.

'What's to be done with the evil ones? Get rid of them? No, because two wrongs don't make a right. Besides, it couldn't be done without a lot of innocent people getting hurt. Like the farmer we have to let them be until the day of the harvest.

'The harvest-time is the end of the world. On the last day God will send his angels to separate the bad from the good. The bad he will banish into outer darkness. The good he will admit to his Kingdom.'

The problem Jesus was addressing was the problem of evil. He wasn't saying that we must not resist evil. Evil must be resisted. But it must be resisted not with evil but with good. Jesus assures us that in the end good will triumph over evil.

The seed growing by itself

'The Kingdom of Heaven is like a farmer who sowed seed in his field. After a while up came the green sprouts. Soon the sprouts turned into sturdy shoots. Then the shoots turned into tall, elegant stalks. And all this was happening without any help from the farmer. The seed was growing even while he slept at night. Finally, it ripened. Then he got out his sickle, and went and reaped the harvest.'

While the previous story shows that there is a power working against us – the power of evil – this story shows that there is an Almighty Power working with us – the power of God.

God has made us his partners. We have a vital job to do – to sow the seed. If we do this, then God will do his part, which is to give the increase.

The mustard seed

'Once upon a time a man planted a mustard seed in his garden. Now a mustard seed is one of the smallest seeds of all. It took a long time for it to come up. When it did, it was so small that he could barely see it. It began to grow, but ever so slowly. However, the man was a patient man. Eventually his patience was rewarded. That tiny little seed turned into a tree. Its berries provided food, and its branches shelter, for whole flocks of birds.

'The Kingdom of Heaven is like that. It begins as something small. But given time, it will become something great. So be patient. Have faith. Don't get discouraged if everything doesn't happen at once.

'In any case, you don't have to be big to have a lot of influence. Take yeast, for example. A spoonful of it will make a whole heap of flour turn into the finest bread.'

We mustn't despise small things and small beginnings. The greatest amount of energy is contained in the smallest particle of matter – the atom. An oak tree begins from an acorn.

The pearl of great price

'One day a man was digging in a field when he found a beautiful pearl. The trouble was the field didn't belong to him. So what did he do? He hid the pearl again. Then he went home and sold everything he had in order to raise the necessary money. Then he came back, bought the field, and took possession of the pearl.

'The Kingdom of Heaven is more precious than the finest pearl.'

Storm on the lake

When evening came on Jesus said to the apostles,

'Let's cross over to the other side of the lake.'

Leaving the crowd there, they got into the boat and set out. Jesus was worn out, so he went to the back of the boat and lay down on some cushions. Soon he was fast asleep.

Suddenly a storm blew up. In a matter of minutes great waves were lashing the small boat, threatening to sink it. The apostles began to bail as fast as they could. But it wasn't fast enough. The boat started to fill up with water. They got really frightened, and thought their last hour had come.

Meanwhile, Jesus continued to sleep as if nothing was wrong. At first they didn't want to disturb him as they knew he needed the rest. But finally, when the situation was clearly out of their control, one of them woke him up. Then they all spoke together,

'Master, don't you care about us? Can't you see we're sinking? We'll all be drowned.'

But Jesus said,

'Of course I care about you.'

Then he spoke to the wind and the sea,

'Calm down! Calm down, I say!'

And just as suddenly as it had sprung up, the storm died down and the sea grew calm.

Boy, were the Twelve relieved! It had been a close shave. But Jesus said to them,

'Why were you so frightened? Is that all the faith you have in me?'

They made no answer. But they were absolutely bowled over by what he had done, so much so that they said to one another,

'Who can he be? Just imagine – even the wind and the sea obey him!'

Madman at large!

They reached the far side of the lake safely after all. But now they ran into a storm of a different kind. As they were getting out of the boat a man came to meet them. Let's call him O'Looney.

O'Looney had been living in a graveyard. The poor guy was covered in sores from cutting himself with stones. He was filthy dirty, and his clothes were in rags. His friends had done everything possible to help him but had failed. Then they tried to keep him tied up so that he wouldn't harm himself or anybody else. But he always managed to break free. He terrorised the whole area, so much so, that people were afraid to pass that way. At all hours of the day and night he could be heard howling and shrieking among the tombs.

O'Looney was insane. He was no longer able to connect with other people. He was completely isolated. Isolation is the greatest human suffering of all. He lived like an animal. He was convinced, and so was everybody else, that he was possessed, not just by one evil spirit, but by several. That's how they explained mental illness in those times.

This was the man who now approached Jesus. Jesus did not back off. He held his ground. Instead of being afraid of evil, it was evil that was afraid of him. Then he began to command the evil spirit,

'Come out of him! You creature of hell, come out of him!'

O'Looney fell on the ground in front of Jesus and screamed,

'Stay away from me! For God's sake, don't harm me!'

This is the typical reaction of a broken, wounded person whose self-worth is nil. What the poor man was really saying was, 'Leave me alone! I'm no good. I'm not worthy of love. I'm evil.'

But Jesus kept on ordering the spirit to get out of him. O'Looney began to quieten down a little. Then Jesus said to him,

'What's your name?'

'My name is Mob,' came the reply. 'There's a whole mob of us in him.'

The devils realised that they were about to be shown the red card. So they asked a favour of Jesus.

'Don't send us out of this area,' they pleaded. 'Let us enter those pigs over there and we'll be happy.'

It so happened that there was a large herd of pigs nearby.

'Okay,' said Jesus. 'If that's what you want, go ahead and enter the pigs. It's about all you're fit for.'

The spirits then left the man and entered the pigs. There were about two thousand of these in the herd, and they took off in a mad rush down the hillside, probably frightened by the screams of O'Looney. And since it's a well-known fact that pigs have no brakes, they plunged into the lake and were all drowned.

Jesus got into trouble over this. However, it wasn't the pigs that squealed on him, but the guys who were minding them. When they saw what happened to the pigs, they took off into town as fast as their legs would carry them. There they told their masters what Jesus had done.

The people came rushing out to see for themselves. But when they found Jesus, it wasn't he but O'Looney who caught their attention. There he was, sitting at the feet of Jesus, fully dressed, looking like a man waiting to collect an Oscar for best actor of the year. They could barely recognise him as the man they had known and feared. They got afraid, afraid perhaps of the powers Jesus had. So they said,

'Leave us alone. Go somewhere else.'

Not as much as a word of thanks for delivering them from a dangerous madman. What was really bugging them, of course, was the loss of all those pigs. How would they get by without their morning rashers?

This must have saddened Jesus but he didn't make an issue of it. He agreed to leave. But just as he was getting into the boat O'Looney said to him,

'Sir, I'm coming with you.'

But Jesus said,

'I've got a better idea. Go back home to your family and friends, and tell them the great things God has done for you.'

O'Looney went off home a free and happy man. He was at peace with himself and with the world. Jesus had not only cured him, but had restored to him his lost dignity as a human being.

Who touched me?

WHEN THEY got back to the near side of the lake, once again a large crowd of people turned up. Never a dull moment. Soon a very worried man arrived. His name was Jairus. When the people saw him coming they made way for him. As soon as he reached Jesus, he threw himself on the ground and said,

'My little daughter is dying. Please come and lay your hands on her so that she may recover and live.'

Jairus was an important man in the area. He was in charge of the local synagogue. It took a lot of humility on his part to get down and beg like that. Obviously Jesus was touched by his humility, because he went off with him at once.

As they were going along a sick woman came on the scene. She had been suffering from a haemorrhage for twelve years. She had spent every penny she had on doctors and specialists. But it was money down the drain, because instead of getting better, she was getting worse. By this time she was on the brink of despair. When she heard that Jesus was in the area, she was determined that by hook or by crook she would meet him. She had fantastic faith in him. She said to her friends,

'If I could so much as touch the hem of his robe, I would be cured.'

Some of them probably thought the poor woman was already a bit touched – in the head – which wouldn't be surprising after all she had suffered. She was a very determined lady. All around Jesus people were pushing and shoving in an effort to get close to him. But this woman was more than able to hold her own among them. By sheer dint of elbowing and pushing, she got right through the crowd and up behind Jesus. As soon as she got near enough, she reached out and touched the hem of his robe. Immediately her bleeding stopped.

Jesus hadn't seen her but he knew something had happened. So he turned to the apostles and asked,

'Did you see anyone touching me?'

One of them replied,

'With all due respects, Master, that's a daft question. Dozens of people have touched you.'

'But I felt power going out of me,' he said.

This shows that every cure took something out of him. Meanwhile, he kept on looking around to see who it was. Then he spotted the woman. She really gave the game away for she was shaking with fear. She would have made the world's worst pick-pocket. Now that there was no hiding, she plucked up courage and admitted what she had done.

'Sir,' she said, 'I'm the one that touched you.'

'Have no fear,' he said. 'It was your faith that cured you. Go in peace. Your suffering is over.'

When the woman came to Jesus, she was looking for a 'quick fix'. But Jesus gave her far more than that. He insisted on meeting her. During that meeting he spoke some lovely words to her. That did a lot more for her than an impersonal, hasty and secretive cure. Jesus didn't just cure a sickness. He cured a sick person.

Why is everybody crying?

Now, WHILE all this was happening, someone brought Jairus the news he had been dreading. 'Your little girl is dead. There's no point in troubling him any further. There's nothing he or anyone else can do.'

Jesus overheard this remark and said to Jairus,

'Don't lose hope. Just keep on believing. Okay?'

Jairus dried his tears and just nodded his head.

Then they set out once more for the house. Jesus now got rid of all the hangers-on. He took only Jairus and three of his friends – Peter, James and John – with him. When he reached the house he found the place in turmoil. Everywhere he looked he saw people crying. As he entered the house he said,

'What's all the commotion about? Why is everybody crying? The little girl is not dead. She's only sleeping.'

They looked at him in disbelief. How could he say such a thing? Some of them treated him as a joke and burst out laughing. He must have got annoyed because he told the whole lot of them to get out. And out they got! He kept back only the girl's parents and his three friends.

Accompanied by these he went into the girl's bedroom. He stood at the side of the bed, looking down at her small, pale, lifeless form for some time. She was only twelve years old. Death saddened him as much as it saddens us. Then taking her hand he said to her,

'Little girl, get up.'

And she sat up immediately. In fact, she got out of bed and began to walk around the room. Jairus and his wife were beside themselves with joy. Then Jesus said to them,

'I want you to keep quiet about this. I mean that. I want no publicity. Now give the girl something to eat.'

Thrown out of his own village

Once Jesus paid a visit to Nazareth, the village in which he had grown up. He brought his apostles with him. On the sabbath day he went along to the synagogue as he always did. They had a custom that if an important visitor was present, they would ask him to read from the Bible and preach. By this time Jesus was famous throughout Galilee, so nobody was surprised when they handed the Bible to him. He picked the following passage from the prophet Isaiah, and read it aloud:

The Spirit of the Lord has been given to me.
He sent me to bring good news to the poor,
to set prisoners free,
to give sight to the blind,
to bring liberty to the down-trodden,
and to announce to everyone a year of the Lord's favour.

This was a well-known passage which talked about the wonderful things that would happen at the coming of the Messiah. When he had read it, he closed the book, gave it back to the man in charge, and sat down. The eyes of everyone in the synagogue were fixed on him. You could hear a pin drop. They had heard about the great things he had said elsewhere. What was he going to say to his own villagers? It had better be something good. Then he said,

'These marvellous words of Isaiah are fulfilled today.'

He started to talk to them. For a while everything went beautifully. They were amazed at the things he came out with. But at a certain point things began to go sour.

'Where did he got all his knowledge from?' someone asked. 'After all, who is he but the son of Joseph, the carpenter.'

'Why doesn't he do here in his own village some of the great things we hear he did over in Capernaum?' another said.

While this whispering campaign was going on, Jesus was sitting there calmly taking it all in. But he could feel their scepticism. He knew he wasn't going to get very far with them. Their whole attitude towards him was wrong.

Then he seemed to lose his patience and said,

'I know what you're thinking. You know all about me. No doubt you will quote to me the well-known proverb: *Doctor, heal yourself.* Well, I have a proverb for you too: *No prophet is ever accepted in his own country.* So your attitude doesn't really surprise me.

'You think, like some other Jews I've met, that just because you belong to God's chosen people, you've got it made. Well, you're backing a loser there. If you want to know the truth of what I'm saying, all you have to do is read the Bible.

'The Bible tells how in the time of the prophet Elijah there was a terrible famine. It lasted for three and a half years, and everybody was starving. Who did God send the prophet to? To a Jew? No indeed, but to a pagan. To a poor widow who was not even living in the holy land.

'There's another example of the same thing. In the time of the prophet Elisha there were lots of lepers in Israel. Elisha didn't cure any of them. Instead he cured a foreign soldier by the name of Naaman. So if you think that you are going to be saved just because you are Jews, you are greatly mistaken.'

On hearing this they flew into a rage. The Kingdom of Heaven was for the Jews, and for the Jews only! Didn't everybody know that? Here was this upstart saying that the Gentiles had every bit as good a chance of getting in as they had. This was heresy!

They had heard enough. A quick nod to the bouncers and out he went – right out of the synagogue. But that didn't satisfy everybody. A gang of bowsies grabbed him, and dragged him off to the top of the hill on which the village was built, intending to pitch him headlong to his death. But it didn't happen because he escaped.

We don't know how exactly he did it. Maybe he put on a display of power and they got afraid of him. Or maybe Peter and his pals came to his rescue, and a fight broke out. Then the local cop was called who got them to cool it. The end of it all was that Jesus slipped quietly away.

Jesus didn't allow this ugly incident to embitter him. He took his light elsewhere. He was more sad than angry. He was sad that because of their lack of faith, he wasn't able to do anything for them. But he must also have been sad to turn his back on his home place like that. As far as we know he never set foot in it again.

Death of John the Baptist

ALL THIS TIME, believe it or not, John was still baptising people. Once he had dominated the scene, and enjoyed great popularity. But now his crowds were getting smaller and smaller. The reason for this should be obvious – Jesus was drawing the people away from him. Those who remained loyal to John didn't like this. They saw Jesus as a rival, and complained to John about it. But he said,

'How many times have I told you that I am not the Messiah? My job was to prepare the way for him. I have done that. Now he must have the limelight. I must take a back seat. But that's okay with me.'

At this time a guy by the name of Herod ruled over Galilee. It was his father, Herod the Great, who killed the babies at the birth of Jesus. He lived in a lonely old castle overlooking the Dead Sea, and was a pretty ruthless character in his own right. When he wanted something he just took it.

Now his brother Philip had a very pretty wife by the name of Herodias. Old Herod took a fancy to her, and married her. John the Baptist told him that this wasn't right. Herod arrested him and threw him into prison. John was held in the dungeons under the castle. For one who was used to the wide open spaces of the desert, it must have been terrible to be locked up in a dark dungeon. But John was tough.

One thing that helped him was the fact that his friends were allowed to visit him. Through them he was able to keep in touch with what Jesus was doing. It sounded great. But it seems he still wasn't a hundred per cent sure if Jesus really was the Messiah. So one day he sent two of his friends to ask him to state plainly whether he was or whether he wasn't. Poor John probably knew that his days were numbered, and wanted to be sure about Jesus.

When the two found Jesus he was surrounded by sick people. As soon as they got a chance they asked,

'Are you really the Messiah? It's your cousin John who sent us. He wants to know for definite. We came right from the dungeon where he is being held at this very moment.'

'You can see the answer for yourselves' Jesus replied. 'Look around you. See what's happening. The blind see, the deaf hear, the lame walk, lepers are cleansed, and the poor have the good news preached to them. Tell John this, and give him this message from me: happy the person who doesn't lose faith in me.'

These were the kind of things that were expected to happen when the Messiah came. John knew this well. So when the two reported back to him, he knew then that he hadn't been mistaken about Jesus.

When they had gone, Jesus began to talk to the people about John.

'Now there's a great man!' he said. 'That's why people flocked out into the desert to see him. He is not like a reed shaking in the wind. He's no softie either. He has lived a hard life. He's a prophet, a great prophet. One of the greatest men ever born. Yet the least in the kingdom of heaven is greater than him.'

The dance of death

Let us now return to Herodias. In spite of her good looks, she was a nasty piece of work. She hated John's guts. Remember, he criticised her marriage to Herod. She made up her mind to have him bumped off the first chance she got. But for the moment she daren't touch him. Herod wouldn't allow it as he had come to look on John as a holy man. From time to time he went down to his cell for a chat with him, even though he found what John had to say disturbing.

Finally, Herodias got her chance. It happened like this. It was Herod's birthday, and he threw a great party. All the big noises were there. Everybody was having a ball. Now Herodias had a daughter by the name of Salome from her first marriage. After dinner Salome came in and danced for Herod. He was so delighted that, without thinking, he said in front of all his guests,

'That was fantastic! I'm so pleased with you that you can have anything you wish. I mean that – anything. Even half of my kingdom. I give you my word of honour.'

The most likely explanation for such a crazy promise is that the old fool was half drunk at this stage of the party. On hearing this Salome said,

'Could I have a little time to think about it?'

'Certainly. Take your time, twinkle toes, take your time.'

She went off to consult her mother.

'Mother, what should I ask for?' Salome said.

This was the chance Herodias had been waiting for.

'Do me a favour, darling,' Herodias answered. 'Ask for the head of John the Baptist on a plate.'

Salome came back with her grisly request,

'Daddy – I mean your Highness, could I please have the head of John the Baptist on a plate?'

Herod was very upset when he heard this, and it put him in a very awkward position. He had grown to admire John, and had no wish to see him killed. Yet he had sworn an oath before all those people. It would look bad if he went back on his word. So he gave in. He ordered one of his soldiers to kill John. The head was duly brought to the girl on a plate, and she gave it to her mother. We don't know what she did with it.

John's was a sad, lonely, cruel death. But it was a holy death because he died for truth and goodness. Besides, his work was done. His friends took away his headless body, and gave it a decent burial. When Jesus heard the news he was deeply saddened. Taking his friends with him, he left by boat for a lonely spot.

An unplanned picnic

However, the people saw him getting into the boat, and guessed that he was headed for a spot on the far side of the lake. So they took off on foot around the northern end of the lake. And guess what? They got there just ahead of the boat. When Jesus stepped out of the boat they were waiting for him.

Jesus might have said, 'Look, I've just got a piece of bad news. I need to be alone. Please go away.' But he didn't. He used his own pain to understand their pain. He looked at these poor people who had such faith in him, and seeing that they were like sheep without a shepherd, had compassion on them. Then he said to them,

'Come to me, all you who are weary and overburdened, and I will give you rest. Learn from me, for I am gentle and humble of heart, and you will find rest for your souls.'

And he began to teach them. As the day wore on the apostles got worried. Finally, Philip interrupted him and said,

'It's getting late. This is an out-of-the-way spot, and the people are tired and hungry.'

'What should we do?' he asked.

'I think we should let them off right now. They can go and buy something to eat in the villages and farm houses round about.'

'Why don't you yourselves go and buy food for them?' he asked.

'For all this mob? It would cost a fortune. We don't have that kind of money.'

Then Jesus said,

'Has anybody got any food?'

'There's a boy here who has five loaves and two fish,' Andrew replied. He must have said this as a joke, or at least with a smile on his face. But Jesus said,

'Get all the people to sit down. Then bring the boy to me.'

It made sense to get the people to sit down. If the crowd heard that grub was being given out, there might be a stampede and someone would get hurt. So they sat down on the grass, all five thousand of them. Then Jesus took the loaves and fish in his hands, and looking up to heaven, said a prayer. Then he said to the apostles,

'Start giving them out.'

The apostles began to distribute the food. Back and forth they went. It was incredible. He was still handing it out. And there was no rationing – everybody got as much as he wanted. A murmur of excitement ran through the crowd. Dry bread and fish may not sound like a feast. But if you were starving, you'd be very glad to have it. When everybody had finished eating Jesus said to the Twelve,

'Now go around and collect up all the bits that are left over. I don't want anything to go to waste.'

They did as they were told and the left-overs filled twelve baskets.

Meanwhile, the crowd was buzzing with excitement. They had seen what Jesus had done. Some of them said,

'This must be the great prophet who was to come into the world.'

Others suggested that they should try to persuade him to become their king. They probably figured that with him as king, they would be a match for anyone, even the Romans.

On seeing the mood of the crowd Jesus got worried. We've already seen how he rejected the idea of setting up a political kingdom. First of all he decided to get the Twelve out of the way. He said to them,

'You cross to the other side of the lake. I'll join you later.'

They left. Then he spoke to the people, and got them to disperse quietly. Finally he was on his own. Worn out, he went off into the hills to pray and to get some rest.

In this great miracle it's not just the power of Jesus that shines out, but also his compassion and generosity. In the world today millions of people are starving. Yet the food is there. Our problem now is not that we are unable to multiply the loaves, but that we are unable to share them.

Saved from drowning

E VENING came on and he was still there. By now the Twelve were about halfway across the lake, but they were finding the going rough as a strong head wind was against them. Darkness fell and it made their task even harder. Jesus knew that with a wind like that his friends would be in trouble. So, forgetting his own troubles (remember, he was still mourning the death of his cousin, John), he went to their aid.

About five o'clock in the morning, just as it was beginning to get bright, he drew near them, walking on the water. They couldn't believe what they were seeing. Someone shouted,

'It's a ghost!'

They were so frightened that they began to cry out. But then Jesus called to them and said,

'Stop acting like a bunch of chickens. Cop yourselves on. It's me.'

Peter wasn't convinced, so he said,

'Master, if it's really you, tell me to come to you across the water.'

And Jesus said,

'Okay, you're on! Get going!'

Peter got out of the boat and began to walk towards Jesus. But he soon got cold feet. Then his courage deserted him completely, and he began to go under. To make matters worse, he couldn't swim a stroke.

'Master, save me, I'm drowning!' he cried out.

At the same time he reached out a hand towards Jesus. Jesus caught hold of his hand and said,

'Peter, how little faith you have in me. Why did you doubt?'

But Peter, who was feeling like a drowned rat, said nothing. Was he glad to get back into the boat! Jesus climbed in after him. Suddenly the wind dropped, and before they knew it, they reached the shore.

A Christian lives by faith. To live by faith means to rely not on our own power but on the power of Jesus. The life of a Christian could be described as a kind of walking on water because, with the power of God, the impossible becomes possible.

Another kind of food

THAT DAY, believe it or not, the crowds were back again. Some people are never satisfied. This time Jesus threw out a challenge to them. 'I know why you're back here today,' he said. 'You're looking for more of the food I gave you yesterday. Now listen well to what I'm going to say. The food I gave you yesterday is okay for this life. But it won't do for eternal life. Another kind of food is needed for that. I can give you that food as well.'

Straightaway some of them began to think of Moses – the man who gave their ancestors a very special kind of food in the desert. It was called manna. So they said,

'Are you trying to tell us that you are greater than Moses? He saved our ancestors from starving to death in the desert. He gave them manna from heaven to eat. What can you give us?'

'It's true that Moses gave them manna,' Jesus replied. 'But in the long run it didn't save them from death. But the food I can give will keep a person alive forever.'

'What kind of food are you talking about?' they said. 'Let's see it. Let's taste it.'

'It's my own self,' he replied. 'My body and blood. *I am the bread of life.* Anyone who eats this bread will live forever.'

The people couldn't stomach this talk about giving himself to them as food. So they said,

'You're talking nonsense. How can anyone give himself as food? It's just not on.'

And they started to leave. Jesus watched them go. Many of them never came back. But he didn't change his teaching to suit them. He let them go. No doubt it hurt him to see them go. When they had gone, he turned to the Twelve and asked,

'What about you? Will you also leave me?'

But Peter spoke up for the rest and said,

'Master, who can we go to? You alone have the message of eternal life. We believe that you are the Messiah, the Holy One of God.'

And Jesus answered,

'I chose the Twelve of you, yet one of you is a devil.'

Jesus was referring to Judas. Even at this stage he knew that Judas would betray him.

The woman who refused to take no for an answer

The crowds were proving to be a big problem for Jesus. Everybody wanted to get near him and to touch him, especially the sick. At times it was so bad that he hadn't time to eat. At other times he was in danger of being crushed. So how did he cope? He escaped! Sometimes he went off to a lonely place. At other times he borrowed a boat and crossed the lake. On at least one occasion he left the country altogether. He went up along the coast to a town called Tyre, about forty miles from Capernaum. Here he was deep into Gentile territory.

He sneaked into a house because he didn't want anybody to know that he was in the area. But somebody recognised him and let the cat out of the bag. Once again it was good-bye to peace and quiet.

A woman came along who said that her daughter was being tormented by an evil spirit. She made up her mind that she would torment Jesus until he cured her daughter. She didn't come up to him and ask quietly. She shouted at him from a distance,

'Son of David, take pity on me! Cure my child.'

But he completely ignored her. However, she went on pleading,

'Please, Sir. I ask you. I beg you. Cure my little child.'

The apostles were mad with her. All this shouting was bound to attract attention. They were probably hoping he would say, 'Drop dead, woman!', and that she would take offence and go away. But he went on saying nothing.

Finally they said,

'Master, for heaven's sake, give her what she wants. Anything to get rid of her and her shouting.'

But he replied,

'How can I? She's a foreigner. I was sent only to the lost sheep of Israel.'

The woman heard this but it bounced off her. She stood her ground and went on begging,

'Sir, please help me! All I ask is this one favour. If you grant me this, I promise not to bother you ever again.'

At last Jesus had to face her. Turning to her he said,

'Surely you don't expect me to take bread that is meant for hungry children and throw it to the dogs?'

A remark like that would have put most Gentiles off. They would have been deeply insulted and gone off in a huff. It was clear that by 'children' Jesus meant Jews, and by 'dogs' he meant Gentiles. But the woman brushed it off, and came straight back with the reply,

'Yes, Sir, I agree the children should get the bread. But what about the crumbs that fall off the table? Surely no one would begrudge those to the dogs?'

What could he do with a woman like that? How could he refuse her after such a display of humility and faith? So he said,

'Woman, you have great faith. Your wish is granted. Go home, your daughter will be okay.'

She believed him and went off home to find her daughter completely cured. How delighted she must have been! All that trouble, all that begging, all that embarrassment, had not been in vain.

The incident tells us a lot about a mother's love. A mother's love is the most reliable kind of human love that we know. The Bible uses it as an image of God's love for us.

Jesus sends out the Twelve

By this time Jesus was involving the apostles in his work. He sent them out in pairs to the villages he himself was to visit. He gave them power to cast out evil spirits and to heal the sick. But their main task was to announce the Good News of the Kingdom of God. They seemed to get on very well because they came back in high spirits.

However, John had a problem for Jesus. He said,

'Master, we saw a man using your name to cast out devils. And since he wasn't one of us, we tried to stop him.'

'You shouldn't have done that,' Jesus said. 'No one who works a miracle in my name is likely to speak badly of me. Anyone who is not against us is for us.'

Thus he gave them a lesson in tolerance.

Then he said to them,

'What are people saying about me? Who do they think I am?'

And they said,

'Some say you're John the Baptist come back to life. Others say you're Elijah, or Jeremiah, or one of the other prophets.'

Then he said to them,

'And what about yourselves? Who do you think I am?'

And Peter spoke up, saying,

'You are the Messiah, the Son of the living God.'

On hearing this Jesus said,

'Peter, you didn't think this up yourself. It was God who put those words into your mouth. Now I have something to say to you. I am going to give you the keys of the Kingdom of Heaven. You are the rock on which I will build my church. The devil will do his damnedest, but will never succeed in tearing it down.'

It's unlikely that Peter understood what Jesus had in mind for him. Nevertheless, the words of Jesus must have given him a great boost. This undoubtedly was a very high moment in his life. But he was to have some very low moments too – as we will see.

The lost sheep

WE'VE ALREADY seen how Jesus went out of his way to mix with outcasts and sinners. The Pharisees were highly critical of him because of this. One day they confronted him about it. But he said,

'So you think I should have nothing to do with these kind of people?'

'That's right,' they answered. 'These kind of people don't give a hoot about the laws of God. There's no hope for them. They're lost.'

'You're right about one thing at least,' said Jesus. 'These people are lost. But surely that's all the more reason why we should try and help them? Suppose a man owns a hundred sheep and loses one of them, what does he do? He leaves the ninety-nine there, and goes off to look for the lost one. And if he finds it, he's over the moon. He brings it home, on his back if necessary. And when he gets home he says to his neighbours, 'I found the sheep that was lost. This calls for a celebration.' And his neighbours will gladly celebrate with him.

'Now if a shepherd will go to all that trouble to find one lost sheep, don't you think it's right for me to go looking for people who are lost? Surely people are more important than sheep. I tell you, there's great joy in heaven when a sinner comes back to God.'

The lost son

The Pharisees still weren't convinced. So he told them another story with the exact same message. This is Jesus' greatest story. Indeed, some regard it as one of the most memorable stories of all time.

'A man had two sons. One day the younger lad got fed up of hanging around at home, so he said to his dad,

'Hey, Dad, how about giving me my share of the property now?'

'Okay, son,' said the dad. 'If that's what you want, you can have it.'

And he gave him what was coming to him, which was a tidy sum. The lad said,

'Thank you, Dad,' and left home and went away to a foreign country.

There he lived it up and splashed his money around. As long as the money lasted, he was not short of friends. But the minute it ran out, his so-called friends disappeared. He woke up one morning to find himself alone and penniless in a foreign country. To make matters worse, a famine broke out.

He hired himself out to a farmer who put him feeding pigs. (The Jews regarded pigs as unclean animals, and so would have nothing to do with them. The fact that the young lad took such a job shows how low he had sunk.) He hated every minute of it. The pay was lousy and the food was worse. He was often so hungry that he ate some of the food the pigs got – potato peels, slops, and all kinds of garbage. This quickly brought him to his senses. One day he said to himself,

'Here I am, making a pig of myself, while back home on my dad's farm the servants are living like lords. Serves me right! What I did to my dad was mean and selfish. I know what I'll do. I'll go back home and tell him I'm sorry. I'll ask him to forgive me and to take me back, not as a son, but just as servant.'

Next morning he told the pigs to go and stuff themselves. Then, having packed his few rags, he set out for home. It was a sad, lonely and fearful journey back. He was not coming back laden with medals and trophies that he could proudly show his father. He was coming back laden with shame and disgrace. What if his dad refused to have him back?

Before he reached the house his dad spotted him coming. What did he do? No, he didn't go back into the house, take down the blackthorn stick, and wait for him behind the front door. He ran out to meet him, threw his arms around him, and gave him an almighty hug! Then he said,

'Welcome home, son! Welcome home! I'm delighted to see you. How've you been?'

'Dad,' the young lad began, his eyes cast down in shame, 'I'm sorry for causing you all this hurt. I don't deserve to be called your son. Just give me a job on the farm, anything, and I'll be happy.'

But the father wasn't listening. Out of his mind with happiness, he said,

'This is a great day! It calls for a celebration.'

Then he said to the servants,

'Quick! Bring out the best robe in the house and put it on him. Put a ring on his finger and sandals on his feet. Then kill the calf we've been fattening, and roast it. We're going to have a feast in my son's honour.'

In no time the party got under way – eating and drinking, singing and dancing. The whole house rang with music and laughter.

Towards evening the older son was coming back in from the fields after his day's work. Hearing the music, he asked a servant,

'What's going on?'

'Your brother has come back, and your father has killed the calf and thrown a big party for him,' the servant answered.

On hearing this he flew into a rage. He was so mad that he wouldn't even go into the house. When the father came out to try to get him to come in, he let him have it.

'I've stayed home all these years. I've worked my guts out for you, and what thanks do I get? Did you ever kill a calf for me? No way. Ah, but when this hobo comes back, only the best is good enough for him! This waster who squandered your hard-earned money on wine and women.'

But the dad kept his cool. He let his older son get the bitterness and resentment out of his system. Then he said,

'Son, you have always been with me, and all I have is yours. As regards the party for your brother, try to see it from my point of view. In spite of what he did, he's still my son. I just had to celebrate, because my son was dead, and has come back to life; he was lost, and has been found."

The story shows that sin is not the road to happiness. Rather, it is the road to misery. But it also shows that if, through human weakness or wickedness, we do sin, we can always come back to God, and he will help us to make a fresh start.

It's the inside that matters

ABOUT THIS time one of the Pharisees invited Jesus and his apostles to his house for a meal. Now there were lots of other Pharisees there also. Before long he got into a fierce argument with them. It started like this. Jesus and his friends sat down to eat without washing their hands. No big deal, you might say. However, for strict Jews like the Pharisees, this was a serious matter.

The Pharisees never sat down to a meal without washing their hands from the elbows down. In their eyes, not to do so was not just bad hygiene, but made a person unclean in the eyes of God. If they happened to have come in from the market-place, where they might have touched something or someone unclean, then they not only washed their hands, but their whole bodies.

That's why they were shocked when Jesus and his friends sat down to eat just as they were. They were determined not to let him get away with it in front of all those people. So they confronted him.

'Why do your disciples eat without washing their hands?' they asked. 'Is that all you think of our traditions?'

To which Jesus replied,

'What difference does it make whether you eat with washed or unwashed hands? Does it make you a better or a worse person? Or course not. All that matters to you, Pharisees, is outward cleanness. You're like white-washed tombs – clean on the outside, but full of rottenness inside.

'Everything you do is done to gain the attention and admiration of others. You love to get the best seats at dinners and in the synagogues. You parade around in public, showing off your long robes. You love it when people salute you. You're nothing but a bunch of show-offs.

'You've got your priorities all wrong. You get all hot and bothered about silly little rules of your own, but neglect the really important parts of God's law – like being just and merciful in your dealings with others. You remind me of a vegetarian who spots a fly in his soup, and immediately calls one of the waiters and has it removed. But when a camel is served up for the main course, he gulps it down without even noticing it.

'It was of people like you that the prophet Isaiah was speaking when he said, "This people honours me with their lips, but their hearts are far from me." '

This was very strong talk, but it was called for. People looked up to the Pharisees, yet they were leading them up a blind alley. The Pharisees saw evil as something which existed outside themselves. But Jesus said that the source of evil is inside us. It has its roots in the human heart. Afterwards he called the people around him to make sure they had got the message.

'Listen carefully,' he said. 'There's nothing that goes into people from the outside, that can make them unclean. The only thing that can make people unclean is what comes out of them. It is from inside people that evil springs. It is there that all evil plans are hatched. From there come things like robbery, murder, adultery, greed, perjury, slander, and all that sort of filth. All these things start inside a person. And these are the things that make a person unclean in the eyes of God.'

How not to pray

THE BIG problem with the Pharisees was that they thought they were the bee's knees. Hence, they despised everybody else. Knowing this, Jesus told them a story.

'One day two men went into the temple to pray. One of them was a Pharisee, the other a tax collector. The Pharisee went right up to the front, where he could be seen by everybody in the temple. He stood there, with his chest stuck out, and started to pray like this:

'Lord, I thank you that I'm not like other people. They are greedy. They are unjust. They commit adultery. I thank you especially that I'm not like that tax collector down there. I fast twice a week. I give a tenth of my annual income for the support of the priests and the upkeep of the temple.' And he went on praying like that for a long time.

'Meanwhile, the tax collector, too, was praying. But he stayed down at the back, and wouldn't even lift his eyes to heaven. His prayer was a very short one but it came straight from his heart. He said, 'Lord, be merciful to me, I am a sinner.'

'Now which of the two made the best prayer to God?' Jesus asked.

'The tax collector,' they answered reluctantly.

'Correct,' said Jesus. 'Those who exalt themselves (that is, put themselves on pedestals) will be humbled. But those who humble themselves will be exalted.'

The Pharisees were raging when they heard this story, because it well and truly knocked them off the pedestals on which they had put themselves.

No figs for the fig rolls

THE PHARISEES had no time for sinners. They believed they should just be written off. Jesus didn't agree, and told them so in a story.

'Once upon a time there was a man who had a fig tree in his garden. He took very good care of that tree. One day he went out hoping to find some figs on it. Alas, there wasn't a fig to be found on it. He was very disappointed because this was the third year that this had happened. He came to the conclusion that the tree was useless. It was drawing nourishment from the ground but giving nothing back. It had to go. It was only taking up space. So he said to his gardener,

"For the past three years I've been coming to this tree in the hope of finding some figs on it, but haven't found any. Don't you think it's high time we cut it down and planted another in its place?"

'But the gardener, who had a great knowledge of fig trees, and was a very patient man, replied,

"Sir, give it one more year. I'll dig the earth around it, and put on plenty of dung. Then, if there are no figs on it this time next year, we'll cut it down." '

The man agreed. We are not told what happened to the fig tree, but it doesn't matter. Jesus had made his point. Just as that gardener was patient with the fig tree, so God is patient with sinners.

Kids' stuff

Another time on arriving at Capernaum Jesus went to a friend's house. The Twelve were about to put their feet up when he said he wanted to see them.

'What were you talking about on the journey?' he asked.

'Nothing, Master, it was nothing. We were just talking,' one of them answered.

'Just talking? It was more than that. You were arguing. I heard raised voices. What were you arguing about? I want to know because I don't want divisions among you.'

'We were arguing about who is the greatest in the Kingdom of Heaven,' the spokesman admitted reluctantly.

'And what conclusions did you come to?'

But the boys were suddenly struck dumb, especially the ones who had been doing most of the talking earlier. So Jesus said,

'Okay, I'll tell you who's the greatest in the Kingdom of Heaven.'

He called over a little child and stood him in front of them. Then he said,

'Get an earful of this. Unless you change and become like this little child, you will never see the Kingdom of Heaven.'

Jesus wasn't telling the apostles to be childish, but to be childlike. He went on,

'Anyone who welcomes a little child like this, welcomes me. But woe to the person who leads one of these little ones astray. It would be better that a millstone be tied around his neck, and that he be drowned in the depths of the sea.'

Millstones were large stones used for grinding corn into flour. If you were thrown into the sea with one of those around your neck, you could kiss the world goodbye. It shows what Jesus thought of those who corrupt the young.

Another day some people brought their little darlings along to meet Jesus, hoping that he might bless them. But the apostles got angry and said, 'This is no place for children.'

But Jesus said to them,

'Don't send them away. Let the little ones come to me. The Kingdom of Heaven belongs to such as these.'

And he laid his hands on them and blessed them.

The man who could show no pity

I T SEEMS that Peter was forever asking questions. One day he came to Jesus and asked: 'Master, if someone offends me, how many times am I supposed to forgive him? Would seven times be about the limit?'

'No, it wouldn't,' said Jesus. 'Nor would seventy times seven times. Listen to this story.

'A certain king called in all those who owed him money. One man came in who owed him £10,000.

"Pay up," said the king, "or I'll have you and all your family sold as slaves."

'The man hadn't a penny to his name but he was a brilliant actor. He threw himself down in front of the king and began to beg.

"Your Majesty," he said. "I'm finding it very hard just now to make ends meet. The wife is in hospital and the children are starving. Please be patient with me. I'll pay you back in time. You have my word of honour".

'The king was a kind-hearted man. He believed the man's story and said,

"Oh, I'm sorry to hear that. Look, in that case, let's just forget it. Go away, you owe me nothing."

"Thank you, your Majesty. The blessings of God on you," said the man.

'On the way out, do you know what happened? You'll find it hard to believe this. The man met this chap who owed him £10. And he said,

"Hey you! You owe me £10. When are you going to pay me?"

"Give me a chance, man," the fellow answered. "It's only a lousy tenner. You'll get your money one of these days."

"I want it right now. And if I don't get it, I'll have you brought to court."

And he began to abuse and threaten him.

'But one of the king's servants had a good pair of ears. He heard all this and reported it to the king. When the king heard it he got very angry. He sent for the man immediately. When he was brought in he said to him,

"Well, of all the low-down creeps! I cancelled the big sum of money you owed me. Could you then not have cancelled the tiny sum that man owed you? Answer me. I want an explanation of your conduct."

'But the man hadn't a word to say for himself, and there was no point in putting on the begging act a second time. The king had him thrown into jail. There he had to do hard labour on bread and water until he had paid back the sum he owed down to the last penny.'

'Now, what does the story tell you about forgiveness?' asked Jesus.

'I suppose it's this,' said Peter. 'If we want God to forgive us, we must be ready to forgive others.'

'And how often?' asked Jesus.

'Always,' said Peter.

'Now you've got the message,' said Jesus.

On the mountain

Jesus' course was leading inexorably to Jerusalem. He knew that the same fate awaited him as befell all the prophets, namely, a violent death. Naturally he recoiled from such a fate. In order to reflect on it and pray about it, he climbed to the top of Mount Tabor, taking Peter, James and John with him. This was a mountain in southern Galilee, about a thousand feet high.

He deliberately chose to go to a mountain. A mountain gives us an overall view, thus enabling us to see the pattern in things. From there things down below can seem very small. A problem which down below seems like an elephant, from up there may seem like an ant. Up there we also feel closer to God. Indeed, we feel we are in the presence of God.

As soon as they reached the top, Jesus started to pray. But the three apostles, tired after the climb, lay down and fell asleep. As Jesus prayed, his face shone and his clothes became as white as snow. Then two very important people appeared to him.

The first of these was Moses. It was he who led the Israelites out of Egypt to the Promised Land, though he died without reaching it himself. The second was the great prophet, Elijah. These two men talked with Jesus about the kind of death that awaited him in Jerusalem.

At some point Peter woke up. When he saw what was happening, he got very excited and said to Jesus,

'Master, it's great to be here. Really great! Why don't we erect three tents here, one for you, one for Moses, and one for Elijah.'

Peter didn't really know what he was saying. He just got carried away. Then a cloud came down over Jesus. And out of the cloud a voice was heard, saying,

'This is my beloved Son. Listen to him.'

On hearing the voice, the apostles threw themselves on the ground and covered their eyes in fear. After a while, Jesus touched them gently and said,

'You can get up now. There's nothing to be afraid of.'

They raised their heads and opened their eyes to find that the cloud had vanished, and Jesus was standing there alone.

As they came back down the mountain he said to them,

'Don't breathe a word of this to anyone, not until the Son of Man has risen from the dead.'

But they didn't understand what he meant when he talked about rising from the dead.

Jesus had a marvellous experience on that mountain. He knew that God was pleased with him, and would give him the strength to face a dark and threatening future.

We too can experience rare moments of light and joy. We get glimpses of the promised land towards which we are travelling in faith. In his love for us, God allows us to taste on earth the joys of the world to come.

Taking the road to Jerusalem

Up to this Jesus had done most of his teaching in his home province of Galilee. He taught not only in the synagogues but in the open – on the roads, in the fields, at the lakeside, in the market-place. But now that the feast of the Passover was approaching, he decided to head for Jerusalem.

Opposition to him had been growing steadily. The Pharisees had hounded him everywhere he went, keeping track of his every word and deed, with a view to bringing some charge against him. But when he took the road to Jerusalem, he knew he was going into the lion's den.

He knew too that life would be difficult for the Twelve. Therefore, he began to prepare them for what lay ahead. He said to them,

'I'm going up to Jerusalem. There I will have to suffer much at the hands of the religious leaders. I will be put to death, and . . .'

The very mention of the word 'death' was too much for Peter.

'God forbid, Master, that anything like that should happen to you,' he exclaimed.

He actually stood in front of Jesus to prevent him from going any further. But Jesus spoke sternly to him.

'Get out of my way, Peter,' he said. 'You're more of a hindrance to me than a help. I have to take this road.'

Then looking around at his disciples he said,

'If you want to be my disciples, you must take up your cross and follow me.'

The man who came back to say thanks

As THEY were crossing the border between Galilee and Samaria, ten lonely, desperate people approached them. They were lepers. They didn't come right up to Jesus, but kept their distance as lepers were supposed to. They stretched out their hands, full of sores, towards him. At the same time they called out to him at the top of their voices,

'Jesus, Master, have pity on us.'

Seeing how desperate they were, Jesus took pity on them and said,

'Go and show yourselves to the priests and you'll be cured.'

They didn't have to be told a second time. Off they went as fast as their wobbly legs would carry them. As they were going along the miracle happened – the leprosy left them. They started to cry with happiness. They hugged one another like footballers do after scoring a goal. Then they sprinted off to present themselves to the priests. These examined them thoroughly, and not finding a trace of leprosy on them, gave them a clean bill of health. That meant they were free to go home.

And that's exactly what nine of them did – went straight home. But one of them didn't.

He realised there was something more important which he had to do first. That was to go back to Jesus and thank him. So back he went, praising God at the top of his voice. Then he threw himself on the ground in front of Jesus and said,

'Sir, I want to thank you from the bottom of my heart for making me well. Thank you, Sir. Thank you.'

Jesus was very disappointed that only one of them had come back to say thanks. He said to his apostles,

'I cured all ten of them, yet only one of them came back to give thanks to God. And that one is not a Jew, but a Samaritan.'

Then he turned to the man and said,

'Get up, and off home with you. It was your faith that made you well.'

It was a very poor show on the part of those other nine. Jesus was disappointed, not so much for his own sake, but for theirs. The fact that they were not able to show gratitude meant they were not fully healed.

Fire from heaven

CONTINUING on their way, they approached a Samaritan village in the hope of finding food and lodgings. However, when the villagers heard that he was heading for Jerusalem, they wouldn't allow him to enter the village.

Those two hot-heads, James and John, took a dim view of this. They felt that Jesus deserved better from them. After all, he had never said or done anything against the Samaritans. In fact, the opposite was the case. He had gone out of his way to be kind to them. So they thought that the least the Samaritans might do was show a little gratitude.

'Master,' they asked, 'Shall we call down fire from heaven and burn them up?'

'You'll do no such thing,' Jesus answered. 'That's not God's way of doing things. Let's just leave them, and go on to the next village.'

As they went along a man joined them and said,

'Sir, I'm ready to follow you anywhere. I mean that.'

Jesus answered,

'I hope you know what you're letting yourself in for. Foxes have dens. Birds have nests. But the Son of Man has nowhere to lay his head.'

Jesus met another man and said to him,

'Follow me.'

But the man said,

'Sir, I will. But first allow me to go back home to say goodbye to my folks.'

Jesus must have known that he was wavering, because he said,

'The man who puts his hand to the plough and looks back, is not fit for the Kingdom of Heaven.'

Another time some people came to him with a friendly warning.

'Leave this place at once. Herod is out to kill you,' they said.

This was the same Herod who had killed John the Baptist. Any threat coming from him had to be taken seriously. Yet Jesus didn't run away. He just said,

'Go and tell that old fox that I'll leave when it suits me and not before.'

Jobs for the boys

WE'VE SEEN how Jesus told the Twelve that he would suffer a lot and be killed. But people hear only what they want to hear. Soon after this, the mother of James and John approached him. She had a big favour to ask for her two boys. She began by bowing low in front of him.

'Missus, what can I do for you?' Jesus asked.

'You know my two boys,' she replied. 'They're two good boys. Any chance you could fix them up?'

'What had you in mind?'

'Like any mother, I want the best for them. I was wondering if it would be possible for one of them to sit on your right hand, and the other on your left hand in your kingdom?'

'My dear woman, you've got the wrong idea.'

'In what way?'

'Well, first of all, what you want me to do is pull strings with God. I know that in this world this happens all the time. But with God this sort of thing cuts no ice at all.'

'That means you can't do anything for them?'

'My kingdom is not about sitting in places of honour. It's about serving others. But let me talk to them.'

Then he turned to the two and said,

'Your mother seems to think that if you follow me, it will be sunshine all the way. What if I were to tell you that it won't be like that? Would you still stick by me?'

'We would, Master,' they answered.

'Right to the bitter end?'

'Yes.'

'Okay, then, if that's what you really want – to be by my side right to the end – you can have it. It's really up to yourselves. But as for places in my kingdom, I don't give them out. That's my Father's job.'

Whatever about James, it seems that John and his mother got the message, because we find them standing near Jesus as he died.

Meanwhile, the others had been listening to all this. They were mad with James and John, and let them know it in no uncertain terms. Their attitude worried Jesus. So he gave them a brief but stern lecture.

'Listen, the whole lot of you,' he said. 'When you look around you in the world, what do you see? You see that everybody wants to be the boss, so that they can lord it over others. My kingdom is not about lording it over others, but about serving others. Therefore, if you want to be great in my kingdom, you must be ready to put others first. Learn from me. I came into this world not to be served but to serve, and to give my life for all.'

How to pray

One day Jesus was praying by himself in a lonely place. After he had finished, his disciples approached him with a request.

'Master,' they said, 'teach us how to pray, just as John the Baptist taught his disciples.'

And he said,

'Okay. First of all, make sure your attitude is right. You must not pray like the hypocrites do. They love to pray standing up in the synagogues and at the street corners. They make sure to be seen by others. But they are not really praying. They are only showing off.

'When you pray, go into your room, shut the door, and speak to God in secret. Even though no one else may see or hear you, God will see you and hear you.

'There is no need to use long prayers. God knows what you're going to ask for even before you ask it.'

'Give us an example of the kind of prayer we should say,' they asked.

And he said,

'When you pray, pray like this:

Our Father, who art in heaven,
hallowed be thy name.
Thy Kingdom come.
Thy will be done on earth, as it is in heaven.
Give us this day our daily bread,
and forgive us our trespasses,
as we forgive those who trespass against us,
and lead us not into temptation,
but deliver us from evil.

'If two of you agree on something, and if you ask the heavenly Father for it, he will give it to you. Where two or three of you meet in my name, I am there with you.'

'But suppose we don't get what we ask for, what then?' they insisted.

'Don't give up just because you don't succeed the first time. Suppose a friend of yours turns up unexpectedly at midnight, and you haven't a crumb of bread in the house, what do you do? You go immediately to the house of a friend to ask for a loaf of bread. You knock on his door, and even though there may be no response from inside, you go on knocking. Finally a light goes on upstairs, a window opens, and he shouts down to you, "What a time to bother me, right in the middle of the night! The door is bolted and we're all in bed. Come back in the morning."

'Do you think you would take no for an answer, go home and, red with embarrassment, tell your guest that you have nothing to give him to eat? Of course not. You would keep on knocking on your friend's door until finally he is forced to come down and give you some bread, not so much because you are his friend, but simply to get rid of you from the door.

'Let it be the same when you pray to God. Keep on asking and you will receive. Keep on seeking and you will find. Keep on knocking at the door and it will be opened to you.

'What would you think of a father who would give his son a snake when he asked for a fish, or a scorpion when he asked for an egg? Not much, right? You wouldn't even call him a father. Now if human fathers, with all their faults and failings, know how to give good things to their children, how much more will the heavenly Father give good things to those who ask him?'

It's dangerous to be rich

Once a young man came up to Jesus, knelt down before him, and asked him a very serious question.

'What must I do in order to gain eternal life?' he asked.

'That's simple,' said Jesus. 'Just keep the commandments.'

'Any ones in particular?' the chap asked next.

'Yes,' said Jesus, 'these ones:

Do not kill.

Do not commit adultery.

Do not steal.

Do not bear false witness against anyone.

Do not cheat anyone.

Honour your father and your mother.'

'Master, I've kept all of those since I was a child.'

On hearing this, Jesus looked at him with love and admiration, and said,

'You still lack one thing.'

'What's that?' the young man asked earnestly.

'If you want to be perfect, go back home, sell everything you own, give the money to the poor, and you will be laying up treasure for yourself in heaven. Then come back and follow me.'

On hearing this, the young man grew downcast. You see, he was very rich, and couldn't bear the thought of parting with all his possessions. So he went away looking very sad. And the interesting thing is – Jesus let him go. He wanted volunteers, not conscripts.

When he had gone, Jesus turned to his disciples and said,

'See how hard it is for a rich person to enter the Kingdom of Heaven. I tell you it is easier for a camel to pass through the eye of a needle, than for a rich person to enter the Kingdom of Heaven.'

This shocked the disciples, so they said,

'That means it's impossible.'

'It's impossible for human beings,' Jesus replied, 'but not for God. With God all things are possible.'

As usual Peter couldn't leave it at that, and asked,

'What about us? We've left everything in order to follow you. What reward will we get?'

'Have no fear,' Jesus said. 'Anyone who has left home, or family, or possessions for my sake, or for the sake of the Gospel, will be repaid a hundred times over here below, and in the next world will inherit eternal life.'

The rich fool

WHEN A RICH person dies, the relatives sometimes fight like dogs over the will. Well, one day a man came to Jesus with a problem.

'Master,' he said, 'when my father died, he left all his money to my brother. I didn't get a penny. Now I don't think that's fair. Tell my brother to give me some of the money.'

'Leave me out of this,' Jesus answered.

'But have you nothing to say to my brother?' the man persisted.

'I have,' said Jesus. 'But it's for you too. In fact, I'd like everybody to hear it.

'Once upon a time there was a rich farmer who had a fine farm of land which produced excellent crops of wheat. Even so, the farmer wasn't satisfied. He was afraid that a drought might come and he would run short of wheat. He wanted to be absolutely sure that he had enought to last his whole life long. So he started to work very hard. He grew more and more wheat until his barn was filled to overflowing.

'You might think that this would satisfy him? Not at all. So what did he do? He said to himself, 'I'll pull down the old barn, and build a new and bigger one. Then, when the new barn is filled with wheat, I'll put my feet up. I'll enjoy myself. Even if a long famine should come, I'll have nothing to worry about.'

'But he never got to build that new barn. God was listening to his plans and said, "You silly man. You may have a mountain of wheat, but you haven't a grain of sense. This very night you're going to die, and all the wheat in the world won't save you. You'll have to leave it all behind you."'

Jesus concluded his story by saying,

'What good would it do you if you gained the whole world but lost your soul? Therefore, beware of greed.'

We don't know how the brothers solved their problem. But Jesus certainly gave them something to think about. People accumulate things and cling to them, because they give them the illusion of security. But security cannot be found in possessions. It can be found only in God.

Rich man, poor man

JESUS TOLD another story about the danger of riches. Here it is.

Once there was a very rich man called Davy who lived in a palace. He wore the most expensive clothes and lived like a lord. Every day was a feast-day for him. Rashers for his breakfast, steak for his dinner, chicken, apple tart and cream for his tea.

And of course a glass of the finest brandy as a nightcap with the last cigar of the day. He never did a tap of work. After all, what are servants for?

'Now right outside his gate lay a poor beggarman by the name of Lazarus. Lazarus was dressed in rags held together with safety pins and bits of string. He was literally starving to death. As a result of malnutrition he was covered with sores. The only friends he had were the street dogs. These used to lick his sores, and lie down beside him to keep him company.

'Every day Lazarus was hoping that as Davy passed in and out, he might take pity on him and give him something to eat. He wasn't looking for a nice leg of chicken or anything like that. He would gladly have settled for the crumbs that fell from his table. But he didn't get them. He looked awful, and was a real eyesore in front of Davy's fine palace. Yet Davy didn't seem to notice him. If he did, he never paid the slightest attention to him.

'Lazarus didn't last long. He died of hunger and disease, and went straight up to heaven, where he got a warm welcome from Abraham, the father of the Jewish people. Eventually Davy also died, and he too got a warm welcome – down below. There he began to suffer terribly. To make matters worse, from where he was, he could see Lazarus up above enjoying himself. One day, unable to stick it any longer, he called out to Abraham for help.

"Father Abraham," he said, "I'm one of your people too. Take pity on me. Please send Lazarus to help me. Ask him to dip his finger in cold water to cool my burning tongue."

'But Abe replied,

"I'm afraid I can't help you. You've only got yourself to blame. On earth you had a good time, but Lazarus had a miserable time. You could have changed all that. It wouldn't have cost you much to give him a crust of bread. It would have meant the world to him. But you wouldn't do it. Now your situations are reversed. He is having a good time, and you are having a miserable time. But there is nothing I or anyone else can do to change it. It's too late. The time for acts of kindness is over."

"Well then," said Davy, "at least do me one favour. I have five brothers back on earth who are heading for this place also, because they are living the same kind of life as I lived. Please send Lazarus to warn them."

"Look," Abe replied, "they have the Bible. They can read it. It's all written down there what they must do."

"Ah," said Davy, "I used to read the Bible every day. But I never really listened to what it was saying. My brothers are no different. Reading the Bible won't change them. But if someone were to come back from the dead, they would get one hell of a fright. They would change their ways, I'm sure they would."

"No they wouldn't," said Abe. "If they won't listen to what God is saying to them in the Bible, they won't listen to someone who comes back from the dead."'

End of story.

Though Davy was very rich materially, he was very poor in another sense. In fact, he was suffering from the worst kind of poverty of all – poverty of heart. His heart was devoid of love and compassion. He was not condemned because he was rich, but because he refused to share any of his riches with Lazarus.

Feathering your nest

HERE IS YET another story Jesus told.

'There was this rich man who had a servant who was a proper waster, and a scoundrel too. When the boss found out about him, he sent for him and said, "Is it true what I hear about you?"

The man made no reply, or if he did, it didn't satisfy the boss because he said,

"I'm afraid you'll have to go. However, before you go, put the books in order."

The servant was a very worried man, and said to himself,

"What will I do when I leave here? How will I be able to support myself? I'm not strong enough for manual work. So digging and that kind of thing is out for me. Begging is out too. I'd be too ashamed for that."

He thought for a while. Then he got an idea.

"Ah, I know what I'll do so that when I leave here, people will welcome me into their homes and give me free food and lodgings."

So what did the scoundrel do? One by one he quietly called in all those who owed his boss anything. To the first man he said,

"What do you owe the boss?"

"A hundred gallons of oil," the man replied.

"I'll change that to fifty," said the servant.

"Thanks very much. That's real generous of you," said the man.

To the second he said,

"And what do you owe the boss?"

"A hundred sacks of corn," he replied.

"I'll change that to eighty."

"Thank you very much. I won't forget you for this," said the man.

And so it went on until he had seen them all. Then he vanished. By the time the boss found out what he had done, it was too late to do anything about it. Naturally, he was very angry. But when he cooled down he said,

"Well, I've got to give him credit for one thing. He certainly knows how to feather his own nest."

And Jesus concluded,

'The children of darkness are wiser in their own way than the children of light.'

Jesus wasn't holding up the wicked servant as a model. He was just making a point. Evil people work very hard, and run all kinds of risks, in order to achieve their evil ends. Good people, on the other hand, often just sit around doing nothing. And for evil to triumph, all that is necessary is that good people do nothing.

Getting a bird's-eye view

People go to all kinds of trouble to see a famous person. They think nothing of queuing up overnight in rain and freezing cold. Here is the story of a man who made quite sure that when Jesus came to town, he would get a good view of him.

Word went out that Jesus was heading for the town of Jericho. The people of the town eagerly awaited his coming. Now in the town there lived a tax collector by the name of Zacchaeus. We already know how unpopular tax collectors were at that time. Well, Zacchaeus was especially unpopular. In fact, the people hated his guts. In collecting taxes from them, he always collected more than the figure set by the Romans. The surplus went into his own pocket. By this time he was a very wealthy man.

The day Jesus was due to arrive, all the people went out to meet him. Even Zacchaeus went out. However, he didn't join the crowd, knowing he wasn't welcome there. So what did he do? He secretly climbed up into a sycamore tree that was growing by the side of the road. He had another reason for climbing the tree. He was a little guy, and figured that at ground level he would see nothing.

They waited and waited. Jesus was usually late because everywhere he went, he was mobbed. It must have been pretty uncomfortable for Zacchaeus up in the tree, but he clung on. It shows how anxious he was to see Jesus.

Finally Jesus arrived. When he came to the tree he suddenly stopped, looked up, and spotted Zacchaeus peeping out from among the branches. Then all the people looked up and saw him. No doubt they were hoping that Jesus would give him a dressing down, that he would expose him for the scoundrel he was. But Jesus did no such thing. Instead, in a friendly tone of voice, he said,

'Zacchaeus, come down from there at once. I want to stay in your house today.'

Zacchaeus couldn't get down off the tree fast enough. The most he had been hoping for was to catch a passing glimpse of Jesus. And now Jesus was coming to his house! He felt honoured, and received him with joy. But the people took a dim view of what Jesus had done. They began to grumble and give out.

'Of all the houses to stay in, he had to pick the house of the biggest scoundrel in town. It's not right,' said one man.

'It's a thundering disgrace, that's what it is,' said another.

And so it went on.

We don't know what Jesus said to Zacchaeus. But we do know this. By the time he was leaving, Zacchaeus had undergone a complete change of heart. How do we know? Because he said to him, right in front of all the people,

'Sir, I'll give half of my possessions to the poor. And if in the past I have cheated anyone, I'll pay him back four times over.'

Then Jesus turned to the people and said,

'I know you were very surprised when I went to stay with Zacchaeus. I heard what you said. Well, today Zacchaeus has been saved. He too is one of God's chosen people. It was to seek out and to save people like him that I came.'

Jesus showed Zacchaeus that he cared about him. Had he avoided or condemned him, the miracle would never have happened. Zacchaeus experienced the love of Jesus. This must have been a wonderful experience for a man who up to this had known only hate. His heart burst into life like a desert landscape after a rainfall.

To be loved in one's goodness is no big deal. It's no more than one deserves. But to be loved in one's sins – as Zacchaeus was – that's magic!

The grape-pickers

By this time Jesus had a large following among tax collectors and sinners. In fact, these were among his most enthusiastic followers. The religious leaders were very critical of the fact that he seemed to have more time for these people than he had for themselves. Jesus replied to their criticisms by telling them a story.

'Once there was a man who owned a vineyard. When harvest-time came along, he needed helpers to pick the grapes. He went out into the market-place at six o'clock in the morning, and found some people gathered there looking for work. He said to them,

'Any of you people care to pick some grapes?'

'What will you pay us?' they asked.

'I'll give you a denarius each,' he replied. (A denarius was the going rate at the time.)

'We'll settle for that,' they said.

And they went off with him into the vineyard and started to work.

He went out again at nine o'clock, and finding others standing idly in the market-place, he said to them,

'If you come and work in my vineyard I'll pay you a denarius. How about it?'

They agreed at once and went with him.

At midday and three o'clock in the afternoon he took on more workers on the same terms. Five o'clock arrived, which meant there was only one hour left, and there were still a lot of grapes to be picked. So out he went once more to the market-place and found some more people there. He said to them,

'Do you mean to tell me that you have been standing here all day long looking for work?'

'That's right,' one of them replied. 'Nobody would hire us.'

'Quick!' said the man. 'Off with your coats and in with you to my vineyard. I promise you I'll make it worth your while.'

And in they went.

When six o'clock came around work stopped. Then the owner said to his foreman,

'Pay the workers. Give each of them a denarius. Start with the last ones I took on, and work your way back to those who have been here since early morning.'

The foreman got the workers to queue up in that order, and the pay-out began. Each one got a denarius. But as the thing went on, an awful lot of grumbling could be heard. By the time it came to the first-comers, the situation was almost out of hand. These came right out and said to the foreman,

'Look here, this is a bum deal! Those first fellows did only an hour's work, yet you gave them a denarius. We've done twelve hours work. We're worn out and sunburnt. Surely, then, we deserve to get more?'

The poor foreman didn't know what to say to them, so he sent for the boss. The boss listened to their complaints, then said,

'Look, fellows, you agreed with me this morning to work for a denarius a day. Isn't that so?'

'Yes,' they answered.

'You've got your denarius, so what's the problem?'

'We still think that we should get more than the others.'

'I know what your problem is,' the boss answered. 'You're angry with me because I treated the others the same way as I treated you. But that's my business. Now take your money, and off home with the lot of you.'

Jesus concluded by saying,

'In the Kingdom of Heaven, the last will be first, and the first will be last.'

A true neighbour

There was this fellow who fancied himself as a bit of a mastermind where God's law was concerned. One day he asked Jesus a question, hoping to show him up.

'Teacher,' he said, 'which is the most important of all God's commandments?'

Jesus replied,

'You must love God with all your heart, with all your soul, with all your mind, and with all your strength. And the second goes like this: you must love your neighbour as yourself.'

The guy must have thought he was a quiz master as well, because he came straight out with another question.

'And who is my neighbour?' he asked.

'I'll answer that one by telling you a story,' Jesus replied.

'A man was travelling down from Jerusalem to Jericho. Now everybody knows how dangerous that road is. It's a muggers' paradise. The man was going along, minding his own business, when some robbers attacked him. Not satisfied with taking his money and valuables, they beat him up, and then the cowards ran off leaving him lying there by the side of the road, half dead.

'Some time after this a priest was passing along the same road. He saw the man lying there, but passed by on the other side of the road. Shortly afterwards a Levite came on the scene. (A Levite was a man who worked in the temple, helping the priests.) He too saw the man lying there, and guess what? He also passed by on the other side of the road.

'Then who should come along on his donkey but a Samaritan. When he saw the man lying there, he got down off his donkey and went over and examined him. When he saw the state he was in, he felt sorry for him. Luckily he knew a little first-aid. He cleaned the man's wounds, poured on oil and wine, and then bandaged them up. Next he lifted the man on to the donkey, and took him to an inn.

"Get a doctor for this man," he said to the innkeeper. "I'll take care of the bill when I get back."

"That'll be okay,' the innkeeper replied."

Then Jesus said to the man,

'Now let me ask you a question. Which of the three acted like a true neighbour to the man who got beaten up?'

'The Samaritan, I guess,' the man answered.

'Correct,' said Jesus. 'Now, go and do as he did.'

To appreciate the force of Jesus' story, we must remember that the man who got beaten up was a Jew, and the man who helped him was a Samaritan. In Jesus' time, the Jews and Samaritans were mutual enemies.

Stone throwing

On one occasion Jesus was teaching the people. He was sitting down and so were his listeners. Things were going nicely until the Scribes and Pharisees appeared on the scene. As usual they came to make trouble for Jesus. This time they really meant business. They were dragging along with them a poor unfortunate woman, whom they claimed had been caught committing a very serious sin.

They stood her right in front of all the people. She must have felt terrible – full of embarrassment, shame and fear. Everybody was staring at her, wondering what terrible sin she had committed. But the religious leaders didn't give a hoot about her feelings. They were using her as bait with which they hoped to trap Jesus.

Without as much as an 'excuse me', their spokesman began,

'Teacher, we caught this woman committing adultery – a very serious sin, as I'm sure you'll agree. Our great leader and law-giver, Moses, said that a woman like this should be stoned to death. What do you say should be done with her?'

They had planned the thing very carefully. He had to answer Yes or No. If he said, 'Yes, go ahead and stone her,' he would lose the reputation he had with the ordinary people as a kind man and a friend to everyone in trouble. Then the people would give up following him. And if he said, 'No, do not stone her,' he would be telling the people to break the law of Moses, and then they could bring a definite charge against him.

That was the trap they had set for him. There appeared to be no way out. But Jesus surprised them by saying nothing. Keeping real cool, he bent down and started writing with his finger on the dusty ground. Nobody knows what he wrote. Maybe he didn't write anything. Maybe he was just playing for time, and merely made some doodles. But the religious leaders weren't going to let him get away as easily as that. They began to badger him,

'Come on, answer our question.'

Finally he stood up very slowly, looked each of them straight in the eye, and then said,

'Let the one among you who has never committed a sin throw the first stone at her.'

Having said this, he bent down once more and carried on writing on the ground. Now the ball was back in their court, and it was their turn to get embarrassed. Was there even one of them who could truthfully say that he had never done a wrong thing in his life? Of course not. Realising they were beaten, one by one, starting with the oldest, they slunk away. Finally, there was no one left but the woman. Then Jesus turned to her and said,

'Has no one condemned you?'

'No one, Sir,' she said shyly.

'Well then, neither will I condemn you. Go away, and do not sin again.'

The woman went away a very relieved person. Thanks to the wisdom and kindness of Jesus, she was free of her sin and of those awful men. How differently things could have turned out! She could have ended up as a bleeding mass on the ground. Who would have benefited from that?

Getting mud in the eye

One day as they were passing along they saw a blind man sitting by the side of the road begging. He had been born blind. The Jews looked on illness as a punishment for sin.

'Who sinned, Master, that he was born like this?' the apostles asked. 'Was it the man himself, or was it his parents?'

'You're wrong,' Jesus answered. 'He's not blind because of sin. He's blind because God wants to show his power through him. I am the light of the world. Anyone who follows me will never walk in darkness, but will always have the light of life.'

Having said this, he took some clay from the ground, wetted it with spittle, and made it into a paste. Then he rubbed the man's eyes with it. (This might seem to us a weird thing to do. But in olden times it was quite common. Spittle was believed to possess curative powers, especially the spittle of a holy person. Certain kinds of clay are also curative.) That done, he said to him,

'You know the pool of Siloam?' (This was a well-known landmark in Jerusalem.)

'Sure,' the man replied.

'Well, go there and wash your eyes in the water.'

The man went to the pool, washed his eyes in the water, and suddenly was able to see. Some of the people who were standing there knew him. But when they discovered that he could see, an argument broke out among them as to whether or not it was the same man.

'Sure, it's the same man. I'd recognise him anywhere,' one said.

'It can't be him,' another insisted. 'It just looks like him, that's all.'

Then the man spoke up for himself.

'It's me all right,' he said.

'Well then, how come you're able to see?' they asked in astonishment.

'A man by the name of Jesus rubbed clay on to my eyes, and then told me to wash in this pool. I did as he said, and suddenly I could see.'

'Where is this Jesus?' they asked.

'I've no idea,' the man replied.

So far so good. But now the trouble starts. It was the sabbath day, and we know that it was forbidden to cure a person on the sabbath. So some people took the man to the Pharisees to lodge a complaint. These asked him to explain what had happened. He did so. Then the real argument began, except this time it was not about the man but about Jesus. Some of them said,

'This Jesus breaks the sabbath. That means he cannot be a man of God. He must be a sinner.'

But others said,

'If he's a sinner, how come he's able to perform a miracle like this?'

Unable to agree, they put it to the man himself.

'What do you think of Jesus?' they asked.

'Oh, I haven't the slightest doubt but that he's a man of God,' he answered.

But some of them still weren't convinced. They even refused to believe that the man had been born blind. So they sent for his parents and questioned them.

'Is this your son?'

'Yes.'

'Was he really born blind?'

'Yes.'

'Well then, how do you explain that he is now able to see?'

'We've no idea. You had better ask himself.'

The truth was – the parents were afraid of the Pharisees. The religious leaders had issued a decree that anyone who openly believed that Jesus was the Messiah would be banned from the synagogue. This was something no devout Jew would wish to happen.

So once more it came back to the man himself. The Pharisees said to him,

'Come on, in God's name, admit it. Jesus is a sinner, isn't that so?'

'Look,' the man answered, 'all I know is this: once I was blind, now I can see.'

'Tell us once more how it happened.'

'I already told you, and you wouldn't believe me. Why do you want me to repeat it? Do you also want to become his followers?'

On hearing this, they flew into a rage and started to abuse him.

'Never!' they said. 'We're followers of Moses. We know for sure that God spoke to him. As for this Jesus, we've no idea where he comes from.'

Now it was the man's turn to get mad.

'That's very strange talk coming from people like you,' he said. 'You ought to know better. A man gives me sight, and you insist on calling him a sinner. Even a child can tell that God does not listen to the prayers of a sinner. Since this man cured me, it can only mean that he's on God's side.'

This really set the cat among the pigeons. The Pharisees now lost their rag completely.

'You've been steeped in sin since the day you were born,' they shouted. 'And you want to preach a sermon to us!'

And they chased him away.

Someone told Jesus what had happened to the man. Figuring that he needed support, he went off to look for him. When he found him he said,

'Do you believe in the Son of Man?' (This was a title for the Messiah.)

'I would believe in him if only I knew who he was,' the man replied.

'You're talking to him right now,' Jesus answered.

When he heard this, he threw himself on his knees, and said,

'I believe.'

Then Jesus turned to the people and said,

'I came to give sight to the blind. I can help someone like this man. He knew he was blind. But I can do nothing for those who are blind and who won't admit it.'

The last remark was intended for the Pharisees.

It has been said that the greatest tragedy is not to be born blind, but to have eyes and yet fail to see. But there is an even worse situation: to have eyes and *refuse* to see. The latter was the situation of the Pharisees.

The good shepherd

There were lots of shepherds in Palestine at the time of Jesus. Theirs was a hard life. When minding their sheep, they couldn't afford to relax for a minute. Since grass was scarce and they had no fences, the sheep were constantly wandering off and getting lost. Consequently, the shepherd had to keep his wits about him at all times.

The sheep had also to be protected from wild animals, especially wolves. Then there were thieves to worry about. These usually came by night, and in some ways were more dangerous than the wolves. Every shepherd carried a big stick with a crook on it. This was used as a walking stick or just for leaning on. It was used to guide wayward sheep and support weak ones. And of course it came in handy in dealing with thieves and wolves.

Many of the shepherds did a first-class job. They really cared about their sheep, and would do anything to protect them from harm and danger. Jesus used the image of a shepherd's care for his sheep to illustrate his care for his followers.

He said,

'The good shepherd loves his work. He owns the sheep, and knows each one of them. He would risk his life to save them from being killed by a wolf or stolen by a thief.

'But how different the hired shepherd is. For him minding the sheep is just a job. The sheep don't belong to him, so he doesn't really care about them. As soon as he sees a wolf coming, he takes to his heels.

'I am the good shepherd. I know my sheep and my sheep know me. I am ready to lay down my life for my sheep. There are other sheep that do not yet belong to me. But one day they will hear my voice, and there will be only one flock and one shepherd.

'It was my Father who put me in charge of the sheep. He is happy that I'm willing to give my life for them. No one can take my life away from me. I give it up freely for the sake of my sheep. But I will take it up again.

'I came that you may have life and have it to the full. This is the task my Father gave me. I intend to see it through no matter what happens.'

A narrow escape

At this a blazing row broke out among the Jews. Many of them were shocked to hear Jesus call God his Father. Some of these said,

'The man is mad. He has a devil in him. We're wasting our time listening to him.'

But others didn't agree and said,

'He doesn't talk like a man who has a devil in him. If he really had a devil in him, how could he open the eyes of a man born blind?'

The ones who thought he was possessed by a devil gathered around him once more and asked,

'How much longer are you going to keep us in suspense? If you are the Messiah, why don't you say so out straight?'

'I told you already but you wouldn't believe me,' he replied. 'If my words won't convince you, then let my deeds do so. The trouble with you is that you don't want to believe. And you don't want to believe because you are no sheep of mine. My sheep listen to my voice. They follow me and I give them eternal life. Not a single one of them will be lost. I'll make sure of that. My Father will help me. He is greater than I am.'

On hearing this some of them took up stones to stone him. But he said,

'You've seen me do many good deeds. For which of them are you stoning me?'

'We're not stoning you because of any good deed you have done,' they answered. 'We're stoning you because you, who are just a man, insist on calling yourself the Son of God.'

'If I don't act like his Son, you don't have to believe in me,' he replied. 'But if I do, then at least you can believe in the work I'm doing.'

Far from being convinced, they tried to arrest him. But he slipped away through the crowd and left the area. He crossed to the far side of the Jordan, and went to the place where John used to baptise people. He wasn't running away. He was preparing to meet the storm which he knew would soon break over him. But even here people sought him out.

'John never did the great things he has done, but everything he said about him has come true,' they said.

And many of them believed in him.

Three loyal friends

JESUS HAD three very loyal friends – two sisters by the name of Martha and Mary, and their brother, Lazarus. They lived in the village of Bethany, which was situated about two miles from Jerusalem. Their home remained open to Jesus when many other homes were closed against him.

Once Martha welcomed Jesus to the house, and immediately began to prepare a meal for him. Instead of helping her with the meal, Mary sat down at Jesus' feet listening to him. Martha got so annoyed with her that she went to Jesus and said,

'Do you not care that my sister has left all the work to me? Tell her to give me a hand.'

But Jesus said to her,

'Martha, Martha, you worry and fret about a lot of things. Yet only one thing is essential. Mary has chosen that one thing, and I'm not going to take it away from her.'

The raising of Lazarus

About this time Lazarus got very sick, and the two sisters sent an urgent message to Jesus. It said something like, 'Lazarus dangerously ill. Come at once.' Surprisingly Jesus didn't drop everything and rush to the house. He stayed on where he was on the far side of the river. Then two days later he said to the apostles,

'Let's go back to Judaea.'

But they said,

'Don't go, Master. It's too dangerous. Only a short while ago the Jews tried to kill you.'

'I have to go,' he answered. 'My friend, Lazarus, has fallen asleep and I must go and wake him up.'

'If he's only sleeping, there's no need for you to go. He'll be okay,' they insisted.

'What I meant was – Lazarus is dead,' Jesus said.

They were completely taken aback on hearing this, and for a while didn't know what to say. But Thomas had a rush of blood to the head and said,

'Let's all go. We might as well die together!'

And they set out.

By the time they reached Bethany, Lazarus had been dead for four days. The house was full of people who had come to offer sympathy and support to the two sisters. When Martha heard that Jesus was coming she ran out to meet him. But Mary stayed where she was. Martha said to Jesus,

'Master, if you had been here, my brother would not have died. But I still believe that whatever you ask from God, he will give it to you.'

Jesus said to her,

'Martha, your brother will rise again.'

'I know he will rise like everybody else on the last day,' she replied.

'I am the resurrection and the life,' he said. 'Anyone who believes in me, even though he dies, will still live. Do you believe this?' he asked.

'Yes, Master,' she said. 'I believe that you are the Messiah, the one who was to come into the world.'

Then Jesus said to her,

'Where's Mary?'

'Back in the house,' Martha answered.

'Tell her I want to see her.'

Martha took off like an Olympic sprinter and when she reached the house she said to Mary,

'Jesus is here! He wants to see you.'

Mary got up at once and went to meet him. All the people who were in the house followed her out, thinking that she was going to the grave. When she reached the place where Jesus was she burst out crying, and falling on her knees, she said,

'Master, if only you had been here, my brother would not have died.'

On seeing her tears, Jesus was deeply moved, and asked,

'Where's he buried?'

'Come with us and we'll show you,' the sisters said.

They set out for the grave. On the way there Jesus himself started to cry. On seeing this some of the Jews said,

'See how he loved him!'

And others said,

'Surely if he could give sight to a man born blind, he could have prevented Lazarus from dying?'

When they reached the tomb Jesus cried again. It was a cave with a big stone at its mouth.

'Remove the stone,' Jesus ordered.

No one moved. Then Martha spoke up,

'I don't know if you realise it, but he's been dead for four days. By now there will be a smell from him.'

But he answered,

'Did I not tell you that if you believe, you will see what God can do?'

A few strong men stepped forward and rolled back the stone. Then Jesus looked up to heaven and said a prayer,

'Father, you always hear my prayer. Hear me now so that these people may believe that it was you who sent me into the world.'

When he had said this he gave a loud command,

'Lazarus, come out!'

Try to imagine the tension of the next few minutes. The people held their breath, eyes glued to the mouth of the cave. Those at the back were standing on their toes trying to get a glimpse of the action. Then a great cry went up as Lazarus came out slowly. His face and body were still covered with the linen cloths the Jews used for burial. There were also bandages around his hands and legs. Then Jesus said,

'Take off the bandages so that he can walk freely.'

I wonder who the brave person was who went up and touched him. I bet it was one of the sisters or, more than likely, both of them.

Many of those who witnessed the raising of Lazarus believed in Jesus. But some still weren't convinced. These went off and told the Pharisees the whole story. The Pharisees got together with the chief priests to decide what to do about Jesus.

'If we let him go on like this, everybody will believe in him,' they said. 'Then the Romans will come and destroy the holy places and our whole nation as well.'

Then Caiphas, the high priest, spoke up,

'Surely it's better that one man should die, rather than that the whole nation should perish?'

The person he had in mind was Jesus. So from that day on they looked for an opportunity to kill him.

No one ever spoke like this

Many of the ordinary people were now saying openly,

'He must be the Messiah. Look at all the wonders he has done!'

However, there was one small problem. Jesus was from Galilee. But it was widely believed that the Messiah would come from Bethlehem, the town King David had come from. They didn't seem to know that Jesus had been born in Bethlehem.

This talk about Jesus being the Messiah worried the Pharisees, so one day they sent some of the temple police to arrest him. When these arrived they found him teaching the people. Seeing how the people were hanging on his every word, they thought it best not to barge in, but to wait until he had finished. So for the time being they stood there at the back of the crowd.

And guess what? Before they knew it, they found themselves listening. They were enthralled by what he was saying. The result was that when the crowd finally broke up, they never laid a finger on him. When they came back without him the Pharisees said,

'Why didn't you arrest him?'

'We've never heard anyone talk like he talks,' they replied.

'Oh, so you too have been taken in by him! You should know better. You're policemen. So cop yourselves on. Just ask yourselves this: Have any of the religious leaders believed in him? Of course not. It's only this rabble that believes in him.'

But they were wrong. One of the leaders did believe in Jesus, but was keeping quiet about it. We've already met him – Nicodemus – the man who came to talk to him by night. He now spoke up for Jesus.

'Surely you're not going to condemn him without giving him a hearing?' he said. 'It's against the law to do so.'

But the others pounced on him.

'You too must come from Galilee,' they said. 'You ought to know that no prophet ever came from Galilee.'

Eventually, they had no choice but to let Jesus be – for the time being.

Kicking up a stink about perfume

Six days before the feast of the Passover, Jesus went to Bethany where they gave a party for him. Martha was doing the serving, and Lazarus, whom he had raised from the dead, was one of the guests. You're probably wondering about Mary? Well, she turned up with a bottle of very expensive perfume. It was the custom to pour a few drops of perfume on a guest when he sat down to table. It was a gesture of courtesy and welcome.

But Mary didn't stop at a few drops. She emptied the whole bottle on the feet and head of Jesus. Obviously, as far as she was concerned, nothing was too good for the man who had raised her brother from the dead. It was really strong stuff. Its fragrance spread quickly through the entire house. Everyone was enjoying it. Well, almost everyone. There was one critic. Surprisingly, it was one of the apostles – Judas, to be exact.

'What a terrible waste!' he exclaimed. 'That perfume must have been worth at least three hundred denarii. (A denarius was a day's wage. So we're talking about the best part of a year's salary.) Just think of it – three hundred denarii gone down the drain! That perfume could have been sold and the money given to the poor.'

But another one of the apostles, John, overheard this remark and wasn't taken in by it. He says that Judas wasn't the least bit concerned about the poor. In fact, he was only thinking of himself. He was in charge of their funds. But he was a thief, and used to help himself to the contributions they got from people. Most likely, the bulk of those contributions came from poor people.

Jesus also heard what Judas said. Turning to him he said,

'Leave her alone. She's preparing my body for burial. The poor will always be with you, but I won't.'

The Jews always put perfume on the bodies of their dead. Jesus was saying that Mary's kind act had another and deeper meaning. Without knowing it, she had prepared his body for burial. Thus he gave a strong hint that his death was very near.

Immediately after this, Judas went to the head priests and made a deal with them. They were only too glad to enlist his help, and promised to make it worth his while. So from that moment on, he began to look for a chance to turn Jesus over to them. Judas didn't suddenly turn against Jesus. There had been a gradual slipping, a gradual dimming of the light, a gradual loss of faith.

Palm Sunday demonstration

AT LAST the day came for Jesus to enter Jerusalem. When he drew near the village of Bethany, close to the Mount of Olives, he called two of his disciples and said to them,

'Go into the village which you see facing you. As you enter it, you'll find a young donkey tied to a post. Untie it and bring it here. If anyone asks you what you're doing, just say that the Master needs it.'

The two set off at once. They had no trouble in finding the donkey. However, just as they were untying it, this guy who was standing there said to them,

'Hey, you two! Where do you think you're going with that donkey?'

But they said,

'Cool it, man! We're not robbing it. The Master needs it. We'll bring it back later.'

And he let them take it.

They brought the donkey to Jesus. Someone took off his coat and put it over the donkey's back, and Jesus got up. They knew then that he intended to ride into the city. His disciples got very excited and decided to give him a hero's welcome. They took off their coats and spread them on the road in front of him. Others took branches from the trees that grew along the roadside, and began to wave them in their hands. Then the whole lot of them started to chant,

'Hosanna to the Son of David!

Blessed is he who comes in the name of the Lord.

Hosanna in the highest!'

Son of David was a title for the Messiah. This shows that Jesus' disciples recognised him as the Messiah. However, in entering the city the way he did, he wasn't living up to popular expectations of the Messiah. Here was no all-conquering hero, riding on a magnificent horse, surrounded by armed troops. Instead, here was a kind and gentle man, riding on a humble donkey, surrounded by friends armed with nothing more lethal than sprigs of palm.

His enemies saw all this, and strongly disapproved of it. Some Pharisees came to him and said,

'Teacher, do you hear what they're saying? Get them to stop this chanting at once.'

'No, I won't,' he replied. 'If they kept silent, the very stones would cry out.'

It was the only time that Jesus accepted hero-worship from the people. He knew that his followers had a right and a need to express publicly their belief in him. Besides, some occasions demand a public demonstration. This was one of them.

He cries over the city

When he came to the top of the hill called the Mount of Olives, he got a magnificent view of Jerusalem, the holy city, dear to the heart of every Jew. He stopped and gazed lovingly at it. Knowing that it was heading for ruin, tears came to his eyes and he said,

'Jerusalem, Jerusalem! I longed to gather your children to myself, as a hen gathers her chickens under her wings, but you refused. The day is coming when your enemies will encircle you. They will destroy you and all your children within you. Yet all this could have been avoided if only you had grasped the opportunity for peace that God gave you.'

Jesus cared about Jerusalem – cared to the point of tears. Yet even he couldn't save it. His prophecy came true to the letter in the year 70 AD. More about this later.

When he entered the city, the whole place was buzzing with excitement.

'Who is this man?' strangers asked.

'That's Jesus, the prophet from Nazareth,' the people said.

Jesus went straight to the Temple. There some sick people came to him and he cured them. But since it was late, he quickly left the city again, and returned to Bethany.

Aggro in God's house

Monday

The following day he came back into the city, and again headed for the Temple. On his arrival there, he looked around at what was going on there. The place was teeming with pilgrims who had arrived for the Passover. Every pilgrim was expected to pay a Temple tax. Those who came from abroad naturally had to change their money to do this. So there were lots of money-changers hanging around the Temple area. These took advantage of the pilgrims, most of whom were poor.

Pilgrims also tried to make a thanksgiving offering. If they could afford it, they offered an ox or a sheep. If not, they offered a couple of pigeons. Here again, the pilgrims were forced into buying, and of course were often overcharged. All this buying and selling and money-changing went on in the courtyard in front of the Temple. The place was more like a market-place than a place of worship.

This is what Jesus saw when he arrived at the Temple that morning. As he stood there taking it all in, he felt anger rising up inside him. All of a sudden, he exploded into action. He made a whip out of cords, and started to drive them all out – cattle and sheep and merchants. He knocked the tables of the money-changers upside down, and coins fell all over the ground.

'Get these things out of here!' he said. 'God's house is supposed to be a house of prayer. But you are turning it into a robbers' den.'

When the chief priests heard what he had done they were furious, and became more determined than ever to kill him. But for the moment they were afraid to take any action against him because of the people. The people listened with rapt attention to his teaching, and presumably would not stand idly by if they tried to arrest him. When evening came on, Jesus left the city and returned to Bethany.

Tuesday

Next morning he returned to the city, and once again headed for the Temple. No sooner had he arrived there than the chief priests and elders gathered around him and began to bug him.

'What authority have you for doing the things you do?' they asked.

'Let me ask you a question,' he replied. 'And if you answer my question, I'll answer your question. Here's my question: Did the baptism of John the Baptist come from God or from man?'

A debate broke out among them: 'If we say it came from God, he will say, "Why didn't you believe him?" And if we say it came from man, we have the people to worry about because they regarded John as a prophet.' So in the end they replied,

'We don't know.'

'Well then,' said Jesus, 'neither will I tell you by what authority I do the things I do. Instead, I'll tell you a story.

The guests who failed to show up

ONCE UPON a time there was a king who gave a great banquet. He invited a large number of people. When the appointed day arrived, he sent out his servant with a message for all those who had been invited,

'My oxen and fat calves are killed. Everything is ready. Come along at once.'

But when the servant relayed this message to the invited guests, one by one they began to make excuses.

'I've just bought a piece of land, and I've got to go and look it over,' one said.

'I've just bought some oxen, and I need to try them out,' another said.

'I've just got married, and am unable to come,' still another said.

And it went on like that.

When the servant reported this to the king, he was very angry and said,

'Quick! Go out into the streets and alleys of the town, and invite in the poor, the crippled, the blind, and the lame.'

The servant did so but reported that there still was room for more. So the king said,

'Go out into the country and the open roads, and bring in everyone you meet. I want a full house. But I assure you: not one of those who were first invited will taste of my banquet.'

The story enraged the Jews. They knew well what Jesus was getting at. The banquet stood for the Kingdom of Heaven. Through Jesus, God had offered the Kingdom to them first, but they had refused to enter it. Their places would be taken by outsiders – sinners and foreigners – who had already shown that they were glad to enter.

Notice that the things which kept those guests from accepting the invitation were not bad things. They were good things. This shows that good things can prove as big a danger as bad things.

Paying taxes to Caesar

The religious leaders had lost that round. But they were a determined bunch. Far from giving up, they went off and put their heads together, not to form a board, but to see if they could get Jesus to say something they could use against him.

At this time Palestine was occupied by the Romans. This meant that the Jews were subject to Caesar, and had to pay taxes to him. They resented paying taxes to a foreigner. As far as they were concerned, they had only one Ruler, namely, God. To him they owed all their allegiance.

The tax to Caesar – that was it! They would ask him if he was for it or against it. If he said he was for it, then he stood to lose support among the people. If he said he was against it, then they could report him to the Roman authorities who would arrest him as a potential rebel. They approached him, fully convinced that this time they had him trapped. They started off praising him, hoping to put him off his guard.

'Teacher,' they began, 'we've got to hand it to you for one thing. You always speak your mind. You are not afraid of anyone. We admire you for that. Now we have a problem, and we'd like your opinion on it. It concerns the tax to Caesar. You know how some people say that we shouldn't pay it, and others say we should. What's your view on it?'

Jesus saw through them at once.

'I can see that you are trying to trap me, you hypocrites,' he said angrily.

When that had sunk in, he said,

'Show me a tax coin.'

They handed him one. He examined it, and then asked,

'Whose head is this I see on it?'

'Caesar's,' they answered.

'Well then, give to Caesar what belongs to Caesar, and give to God what belongs to God.'

There are some things which believers can give to Caesar, that is, to the secular powers. But there are other things which should be given only to God.

A widow's mighty mite

JESUS SPENT most of the day debating with his enemies in and around the Temple. At one point he decided to take a break from it all. He sat down on the steps near one of the gates of the Temple. There was a collection box nearby. Visitors to the Temple put money into the box, and this money was used for the upkeep of the Temple.

As he sat there he watched people putting money into the box. He noticed that some rich people made very generous offerings. Then a poor widow came along. She stopped by the box, took out a small purse, and opened it. Then she turned it upside down and shook it. Out came a penny. She took the penny and dropped it into the box.

Most people would say, 'Those rich people are great people. See the large offerings they make. As for that little old lady, she should be told to keep her miserable penny.' But this is not how Jesus saw it. He never judged by appearances. He always looked at the heart. He was so impressed by the offering of the widow that he drew the attention of his disciples to it.

'That widow put in more than any of the others,' he said.

'How do you make that out?' they asked.

'Look at it this way.' he replied. 'It's true that the others gave more than her. But they won't miss what they gave. They have plenty left. But she gave everything she had. No one can give more than that.'

It's not the size of the offering that matters, but the cost of it. It's not the end result that matters, but the effort made and the spirit shown.

The destruction of Jerusalem foretold

THAT EVENING, as they were leaving the Temple, one of his disciples said to him,' What wonderful stones, and what a wonderful building!'
'Believe me,' Jesus replied, 'it will all be torn down. There won't be left a stone upon a stone.'

A short while later he and his apostles sat down on the Mount of Olives. The temple was directly opposite them, its golden dome reflecting the rays of the setting sun. It was terrible to think that this beautiful and sacred building would be destroyed.

'When will this happen?' the apostles asked.

'It will happen in this generation,' he replied.

'Will it be bad?'

'It will very bad. When the time comes, anyone who can get out should do so as quickly as possible. If someone is working in the fields, he shouldn't even stop to pick up his coat. If someone is on the roof, he shouldn't even go back inside his house but head for the hills immediately. It will be especially hard on mothers with little children. Pray that it doesn't happen in winter time.'

How right Jesus was. Jerusalem was destroyed by the Romans in the year 70 AD after a long siege. Josephus, a historian of that time, says that over a million people were killed or died of starvation during the long siege. The Temple was burned to the ground. Today all that's left of it is part of the western outer wall, which is known as the Wailing Wall.

Do not be afraid

AT THE SAME time Jesus warned his disciples that rough times lay ahead for them. He said,
'You will be dragged before kings and rulers. You will be imprisoned, tortured, and some of you will be killed. When they bring you to court, don't worry beforehand

about how to defend yourselves. I myself will put words in your mouth so that you will be more than a match for your accusers.

'As for your lives – don't worry either. Are not sparrows sold two for a penny? Yet not a single one of them falls to the ground without your heavenly Father noticing it. So don't be afraid. You are worth more than many sparrows. Even the hairs of your head are counted.

'Anyone who acknowledges me before others, I will acknowledge before my Father in heaven. But anyone who is ashamed of me before others, I will be ashamed of that person before my Father in heaven.

'But there will also be people who will welcome you. Anyone who welcomes you, welcomes me. And anyone who welcomes me, welcomes the Father who sent me. I give you my word of honour: If anyone gives you a cup of cold water because you are disciples of mine, that person will not go without a reward.'

The talents

Here is another story Jesus told which seems to have been aimed at everybody.

'Once upon a time there was a man who went on a long trip abroad. Before leaving he called in three of his servants, and gave each of them a sum of money. Each was given according to his ability. The first got £5,000, the second £2,000, and the third £1,000. He said to them,

"Put the money to good use, and see what profit you can make between now and the time I get back."

'Then he departed without telling them exactly how long he was going to be away.

'The man who got £5,000 set to work at once. He started up a business, worked very hard, and succeeded in doubling the money. The man who got £2,000 did the same, and he also doubled his money. But the man who got £1,000 didn't put the money to any use at all. He just dug a hole in the ground and buried it.

'The boss was away a long time. When at last he got back, he called in the three servants and asked them how they had got on. The first man said,

"Sir, you remember you gave me £5,000?"

"I remember," the boss answered, "and what did you do with it?"

"I started up a business and made another £5,000."

"Well done!" said the boss. "You're a good and reliable servant. Because you have shown that you can be trusted with a comparatively small sum of money, I'm going to put you in charge of a really big sum. Now come inside. I've a treat in store for you."

The second man came in. Again it was good news all the way.

"Sir," he said, "you gave me £2,000. I did some business with it and doubled it."

"Well done!" said the boss. "You have proved that you are a reliable servant. I've got big plans for you. Come inside, and I'll tell you all about them."

'Finally, in came the third man.

"Sir," he said, "here's your money back."

"Wait a minute!" said the boss. "That wasn't the idea. You were supposed to try to make a profit with it."

"I realise that, but knowing that you are a hard man to satisfy, I was afraid," the servant said.

"So what did you do with it?"

"I hid it, Sir."

"You're a lazy, good-for-nothing servant. The very least you might have done was to put the money in a bank. That way it would have earned some interest. But obviously even that was too much for you. Give me the money. Now pack your bags and get out of here. I'll give the money to one of the others who will make good use of it." '

God gives different talents to different people. A talent has first of all to be recognised. Then it has to be developed and put to use. Life is God's gift to us. What we do with life is our gift to God.

The Last Judgement

JESUS ALSO spoke to his disciples about the great settling of accounts which will take place on the last day. He said,

'On the last day the Son of Man will come in all his glory, with an escort of angels. He will sit down like a king on a high throne. All the peoples of the world will be gathered before him. Then he will separate the good from the bad like a shepherd separates the sheep from the goats. He will put the good on his right-hand side, and the bad on his left- hand side.

'Then he will say to the good,

"Come, my friends, enter the kingdom God has prepared for you since the beginning of the world. For I was hungry and you gave me food; I was thirsty and you gave me a drink; I was a stranger and you welcomed me; I was naked and you gave me clothes; I was sick and you looked after me; I was in prison and you visited me."

'The good will be surprised to hear all this and will ask, "Lord, when did we see you hungry and feed you, or thirsty and give you a drink, or a stranger and welcome you, or naked and give you clothes, or sick and look after you, or in prison and visit you?"

'And the King will answer,

"I assure you that as long as you did it to the least of my brothers and sisters, you did it to me."

'Then he will turn to those on his left and say,

"Depart from me. For I was hungry and you didn't give me food; I was thirsty and you didn't give me a drink; I was a stranger and you didn't welcome me; I was naked and you didn't give me clothes; I was sick and you didn't look after me; I was in prison and you didn't visit me."

'They will ask in surprise,

"Lord, when did we see you hungry or thirsty, a stranger or naked, sick or in prison, and refuse to help you?"

'And he will answer,

"As long as you didn't do it to one of the least of my brothers and sisters, you didn't do it to me."

This is one of the most revolutionary parts of the Gospel. It is also one of the most disturbing. Many Christians think that as long as they don't do any harm to anyone, they have done all that is expected of them. Jesus wants his disciples to open their hearts to the needs of others. Even though this is not easy, it is a call to life. Because to open one's heart is to begin to live.

The calm before the storm

Spy Wednesday

It seems that Jesus didn't show up at all in the city on Wednesday. Instead, he had a quiet day in Bethany with his friends. It was the calm before the storm. But his enemies were busy. They called a top-level meeting to plan their tactics. The meeting took place in the palace of Caiphas, the high priest. The plan they came up with was to kill Jesus quietly. However, they decided not to do it during the feast, in case it might cause a riot among the people.

At some point Judas approached them and said,

'How much will you give me if I hand him over to you?'

'We'll give you thirty silver pieces,' they said.

Even in those days thirty silver pieces wasn't a big sum of money. It was only the price paid to buy the freedom of a slave. Judas accepted. From that moment on he was on the look-out for an opportunity to betray Jesus.

The Last Supper

Thursday

It was the eve of the feast of the Passover. The Passover was the feast in which the Jews relived the greatest event in their history – the Exodus, or the escape from Egypt. It was the dream of every devout Jew to celebrate the Passover at least once in his life in the holy city of Jerusalem.

That morning Jesus said to Peter and John,

'Go and make the necessary preparations so that we can eat the Passover meal.'

'Where do you intend to eat it?' they asked.

Obviously Jesus had already made arrangements because he said to them,

'Go into the city. There you will meet a man carrying a jar of water. Follow him. He will lead you to a certain house. When you get there, say to the owner, "The Master wants to know if the room is ready in which he is to eat the Passover meal with his friends." He will show you a large room. Get it ready.'

They left at once for the city. There they found everything just as Jesus had said, and made the necessary preparations for the meal.

The washing of the feet

That evening Jesus slipped into the city unnoticed, and sat down to table with the apostles. Judas was there too. And, surprisingly, none of the other apostles knew what he was planning. But Jesus knew. At the start of the meal he said,

'You've no idea how much I have longed to eat this meal with you before I suffer.'

He got up from the table, took off his outer robe, and put on an apron. Then he took a towel and a basin of water, and started to wash their hot and dusty feet. This job was usually done by the lowest servant in the house. Peter thought that Jesus was lowering himself too much, so when his turn came to have his feet washed, he said,

'Hold it, Master! I won't allow this.'

But Jesus answered,

'I know that you don't understand now why I'm doing it. But you'll understand later.'

However, Peter dug in.

'You'll never wash my feet,' he said.

On hearing this, Jesus said,

'Peter, get this straight. If you will not allow me to wash your feet, then I'm finished with you.'

This shook Peter. So he said at once,

'In that case you can wash not just my feet, but my hands and face as well.'

'That's not necessary,' said Jesus. 'The person who has had a bath lately needs only to wash his feet, and he is clean all over. But not all of you are clean.'

They didn't understand at the time what he meant by 'not all of you are clean'. It was meant for Judas. All this time he was sitting there pretending nothing. Unlike Peter, when his turn came to have his feet washed, he kept his mouth shut. But Jesus knew that he wasn't clean where it really mattered, namely, in his mind and heart. Inside he was full of treachery and deceit. Jesus was letting him know that he knew what he was up to, hoping that it might cause him to change his mind while there was still time.

When Jesus had finished washing their feet, he put on his robe and sat down to table again. Then he said,

'You're still wondering why I did this. I'll explain why. You call me "Master", and rightly so. I am your Master. I have given you an example. If I, your Master, have washed your feet, surely then you should be willing to wash one another's feet?'

In a nutshell, he was giving them a practical demonstration of how they were to treat one another. It was especially aimed at those who would have positions of authority in the community. The latter should see their office, not as a chance to be served, but to serve.

Talking about the traitor

After this Jesus got very upset. What upset him was the fact that one of the Twelve (Judas) was about to betray him. Jesus had personally chosen and trained Judas. Judas had heard all his teaching and witnessed all his miracles. He was one of the inner circle. Yet now he was about to betray him. The treachery of a friend is far more hurtful and difficult to deal with than the treachery of an enemy. Jesus looked at the Twelve and said sadly,

'One of you is about to betray me.'

Now it was the turn of the apostles to get upset. It grieved them to think that one of their number could do such a thing. One after another they began to ask,

'Is it I, Master?'

Taking a piece of bread, Jesus said,

'It is the man to whom I will give this piece of bread. The man who betrays me is doing a terrible thing. It would be better for him if he had never been born.'

The apostles were now more upset than ever. But they were no nearer to guessing who the traitor was. John was sitting next to Jesus. Peter signalled to him to ask once more. So John said to Jesus,

'Master, tell us who it is.'

Jesus didn't answer. Instead, he dipped a piece of bread in the dish, and handed it to Judas. (The act of offering a piece of bread dipped in the dish was a gesture of courtesy, a bit like our gesture of pouring a drink for an honoured guest.)

Then he said to him,

'Be quick about what you're going to do.'

Judas got up from the table and left the room. Jesus knew well where he was going. But the others still didn't suspect that Judas was the one. He was in charge of the money box. Consequently, they thought that Jesus had said to him, 'Go and buy what we need for the feast.'

By this time night had fallen. Judas went out into the darkness. But darkness was nothing new to him. The day he decided to betray Jesus, he left the light and passed into darkness.

Jesus let Judas know that he knew what he was up to. Yet he refused to expose him in front of the others. In refusing to point the finger at him, he gave him an opportunity to change his mind. Jesus never rejected Judas. On the contrary, he loved him to the end.

What Judas did hurt the apostles too. After all, he was one of themselves. They had trusted him, and shared everything with him. They thought they knew him, and yet he turned out to be a traitor. In betraying Jesus he betrayed them too.

Instituting the Eucharist

During the supper, Jesus took a cake of the unleavened bread. Having said a prayer over it to bless it, he broke it into pieces, and gave each of them a piece, saying, 'Take this, all of you, and eat it; this is my body which will be given up for you.'

Next he took a cup filled with wine. Again he thanked God, blessed it and gave it to them, saying,

'Take this, all of you, and drink from it; this is the cup of my blood, the blood of the new and everlasting covenant. It will be shed for you and for all so that sins may be forgiven.'

He was telling them that his body would be broken, and his blood would be shed for them. And not just for them, but for everyone everywhere.

When they all had drunk from it, he said,

'Do this in memory of me.'

A new commandment

HAVING SHOWN them how much he loved them, he went on to talk about how he wanted them to love one another.

'I have a new commandment to give you,' he said. 'Love one another as I have loved you. People will recognise you as disciples of mine if you love one another. The greatest proof of love that anyone can give is when he is ready to die for his friends. And you are my friends. I no longer call you my servants. I call you my friends. Remember, you did not choose me; it was I who chose you.

'You and I are like a vine. I am the trunk of the vine; you are the branches. Any branch that is cut off from the vine withers away. So, separated from me, you can do nothing. But united with me, you will bear much fruit.

'As the Father has loved me, so I have loved you. I have told you this so that my joy may be in you. This is my commandment: love one another, as I have loved you. '

Peter's denial foretold

A LITTLE WHILE later Jesus said,
'Tonight you will all lose faith in me. You will be scattered like sheep are when the shepherd is struck down. Each of you will go his own way, and I will be left alone. But I am not alone, because the Father is with me.'

The apostles didn't like to hear Jesus say that they would all leave him, least of all Peter. He began to tell Jesus that he was ready to stick by him through thick and thin.

'Master, you can count on me,' he said.

'Can I?' said Jesus, looking directly at him.

'You can,' Peter replied. 'Even if all the others should abandon you, I will never abandon you.'

Brave words! But Jesus wasn't taken in by them. He knew Peter better than Peter knew himself. So he said,

'Are you sure about that?'

'Absolutely sure. I'm ready to go to prison, even to die for you, if necessary.'

'Peter, you don't know what you're talking about. Before the cock crows tomorrow morning, you will have denied me three times.'

Poor Peter got terribly upset on hearing this. But Jesus added a word of encouragement. He said,

'Peter, Satan is out to get you. But I have prayed for you that your faith may not fail. When you have recovered, I want you to strengthen the others.'

Breaking up is never easy

JESUS KNEW that his death would come as a terrible blow to his apostles. Their faith in him and in God would be tested to its foundations. So he tried to prepare them for it, and at the same time to comfort them. He said,

'Do not let your hearts be troubled or afraid. No matter what happens, keep on trusting in God and in me. It was from the Father that I came out when I entered this world. Now I am leaving the world and going back to the Father. My Father's house has many rooms. I will reserve a place for you, so that where I am you also may be. You know the way to where I'm going.'

'We don't,' said Thomas. 'We don't even know where you're going, so how could we know the way there?'

Jesus replied,

'Thomas, I am the way. No one can come to the Father except through me.'

At this point Philip butted in,

'Master, let us see the Father. Just give us one glimpse of him, and we'll be happy.'

'Philip, you've already seen him,' Jesus replied.

'I'm afraid I don't follow you,' Philip said.

'Philip, do you mean to tell me that you have been with me all this time, and you still don't know who I am? Do you not realise that to see me is to see the Father? That's how close we are.'

It's doubtful if Philip understood this, but he didn't ask any more questions. Maybe he didn't want to appear stupid in front of the others.

I will not leave you orphans

THEN JESUS SAID, 'Peace I leave with you, my own peace I give you. A peace which the world cannot give, this is my gift to you. So do not let your hearts be troubled or afraid. You are sad because I told you that I'm leaving you. But I will return. You will see me again, and your sorrow will be turned into joy, and that joy no one will be able to take from you.

'I will not leave you orphans. I will ask my Father, and he will send you the Holy Spirit. The Holy Spirit will guide you into the truth, and stay with you forever. It is for your own good that I go, because if I did not go, the Spirit would not come.'

Once again he spoke to them about the rough times that lay ahead for them.

'Servants are not greater than their master,' he said. 'If they persecuted me, they will also persecute you. They will expel you from the synagogues. Indeed, the hour is coming when anyone who kills you will think he's honouring God.

'I'm telling you all this, so that your faith may not be shaken. When it happens, remember that I foretold it. The world will inflict a lot of suffering on you. But be brave. I have overcome the world.'

Then, rising from table, he said,

'It's time to be going from here. Get up, let us be on our way.'

They left the supper room, made their way quietly out of the city, and climbed the slopes of the Mount of Olives. They were heading for a garden where Jesus had often gone to rest and to pray. It was called The Garden of Gethsemane. The spot was well known to Judas. He knew that this was where he would find Jesus. It was an ideal place in which to arrest him.

The agony in the garden

When they reached the garden Jesus said to the apostles,

'You stay here, I'm going over there to pray.'

But he took Peter, James and John with him. The same three who were privileged to share his hour of glory on Mount Tabor, were now being called upon to share his hour of weakness. All of a sudden a terrible sadness came over him, and he said to the three,

'I'm ready to die with sorrow. Stay awake and watch with me.'

Then, going a little distance from them, he threw himself face downwards on the ground, and started to pray.

'My Father,' he said, 'all things are possible to you. Take this cup away from me. Yet, if you want me to drink it, I will.'

The Jews looked on life as a cup which contains a mixture of sweet things and bitter things. Jesus' cup was now brimming over with bitter things.

After a while he came back to the three and found them asleep. It was a poor show on their part. It wasn't that they didn't know what he was going through. They did. Besides, he has specifically asked for their support.

How many times he had come to their aid in their moments of need. And the one time he asked them for help, they failed him miserably. They left him to drink the cup of sorrow alone. He was disappointed in them, especially in Peter. He let him know this. Waking him up, he said to him,

'I thought you said you were ready to die for me? Now you can't stay awake even one hour for me! Watch and pray. I know that the spirit is willing, but the flesh is weak.'

He went away and prayed again,

'My Father, if I have to drink this, then may your will be done.'

After a while he came back to the three, and again found them sleeping. This time he didn't even wake them up. He let them sleep on and returned to his prayer.

The loneliness of the struggle now really got to him. He prayed all the harder, the same prayer as before. The agony almost crushed him. He did not want to die, least of all to die a violent death at the hands of his enemies. He struggled so hard with it that sweat ran down his face like drops of blood falling on the ground.

Eventually he found the strength to face what had to be faced. Courage is not never being afraid. It is being afraid, and overcoming it, or continuing on in spite of it. Returning to the three, Jesus said,

'There you are! Still sleeping! Get up at once. The hour has come. My betrayer is close at hand.'

The arrest

AT THAT very moment lights appeared at the end of the garden. Then Judas, the traitor, arrived on the scene. With him was a band of men armed with swords and clubs. Some of them carried lanterns, more of them torches. They were made up of Temple guards and Roman soldiers, and had been sent by the chief priests. Though it was dark in the garden, Judas had no trouble picking Jesus out. He had already told the others,

'Look out for the man I kiss. As soon as I kiss him, grab him.'

He probably thought that by greeting Jesus with a sign of friendship, he would put him off his guard. Anyway, he went up to Jesus and said,

'Greetings, Master!' Then he kissed him.

Jesus said to him,

'Judas, my friend, do you betray the Son of Man with a kiss?'

By addressing Judas in this way, Jesus made one last effort to reach him. But Judas was past the point of rescue. He made no answer. Instead, he stepped aside to let the soldiers at Jesus. But to his surprise not one of the mob made any move to arrest him. Jesus then came forward to meet them and said,

'Who are you looking for?'

'Jesus of Nazareth,' they answered.

'I am Jesus of Nazareth,' he said calmly.

When they heard him say this with such calm courage, they got afraid of him. Those at the front drew back in fear, and in the darkness fell over those behind. Again he asked,

'Who are you looking for?'

'Jesus of Nazareth,' they replied.

'I've just told you that I am Jesus of Nazareth. If it's me you're looking for, then let the others go free.'

This shows how Jesus cared about his friends even when he himself was in mortal danger.

Now, at last, a couple of them plucked up courage, stepped forward and grabbed him. He did not resist. But Peter just couldn't stand there and watch his Master being taken away like that. In a fit of reckless courage, he drew his sword and made a swipe at one of them. It turned out to be a servant of the high priest, a man by the name of Malchus. The blow left the guy's right ear hanging off. But Jesus didn't agree with violence, so he said to Peter,

'Put away your sword. Those who live by the sword will die by the sword.'

Then he went over to Malchus, touched his ear, and it healed up at once.

Then Jesus said to the men who arrested him,

'What are the clubs and swords for? What do you take me to be? A bandit or something? Why didn't you arrest me in the Temple? Day after day I taught there openly, and you never laid a hand on me. But now you come under cover of darkness. Indeed, this is the hour of the Powers of Darkness.'

By this he meant that there was a greater evil at work that night. That, in fact, the whole Powers of Hell were let loose against him.

Then he surrendered himself to them. All the apostles deserted him and ran away. But there was one young lad who followed on behind at what he thought was a safe distance. All he had on him was a linen sheet. Maybe it was the white sheet that gave him away, because someone spotted him and made a grab at him. But the young lad must have been quick on his feet because all they caught was the linen sheet. This ripped off and the lad ran away naked. It is believed that he was a disciple by the name of Mark, who later wrote one of the Gospels.

Trial before Annas

JESUS HAD to go through not one trial, but about six. He was now surrounded by his enemies. There was no one to speak for him or to defend him. He was completely on his own.

They took him first of all to the house of Annas, keeping his hands tied behind his back. Annas was the ex-high priest. Though the Romans had sacked him from his job, he still acted as though he held the office. It was he who earlier had advised the religious leaders that Jesus should die.

It was about midnight when Jesus was brought before Annas. Annas began to question him.

'Tell me about your teaching and your followers,' he asked.

'You should know the answer to that question yourself,' Jesus replied. 'I didn't teach in some secret place. I taught in the open – in the synagogues and in the temple. If you really want to know what I taught, ask the people who heard me. They'll tell you what I said.'

One of the officers thought this a cheeky answer.

'How dare you answer the high priest like that!' he said. And he hit Jesus a blow across the face with his hand.

But Jesus said,

'If what I've said is a lie, prove it. If I'm telling the truth, why did you hit me?'

Annas realised that he wasn't getting anywhere with Jesus, so, since time was limited, he sent him, still bound, to the real high priest – Caiphas.

Before Caiphas and the council

It wasn't just Caiphas that Jesus now faced, but the whole council of religious leaders. Several witnesses were produced. However, it was obvious that they were lying because they contradicted one another. But this didn't worry the religious leaders unduly. Now that they had him in their grasp, they were determined to kill him by fair means or foul.

Still, no matter how hard they tried to pin some charge on him, nothing would stick. The charges were so ridiculous that Jesus scarcely had to defend himself. He just let the witnesses go on contradicting one another.

Finally, however, these two guys came forward and said,

'We heard him say that he would destroy the Temple and rebuild it in three days.'

Jesus made no reply to this either. Then Caiphas, who was getting increasingly impatient, stood up and said to him,

'How can you stand there and listen to all these accusations without replying?'

Jesus still would not reply. Then Caiphas put him under oath to answer. He said,

'I'm now asking you in God's Name to tell us if you are the Messiah, the Son of God?'

Jesus now did reply.

'You've just said what I really am,' he answered. 'But you don't know the full truth. Hereafter you will see the Son of Man seated in power and coming in the clouds of heaven.'

This proved too much for Caiphas. To show what he thought of what Jesus had said, he stood up and tore his robe in two. Then he shouted,

'He has blasphemed! You've all heard him. Gentlemen, what is your verdict?'

'He deserves the death penalty,' they answered with one voice.

Then all their hatred poured out. They started to abuse him. They punched him, and spat on him. Next they blindfolded him. Then, taking turns, they struck him on the face and said,

'If you really are the Messiah, then tell us who struck you.'

But Jesus made no reply.

Peter's denials

WE SAW how all the apostles ran away when Jesus was arrested. Well two of them, Peter and John, had second thoughts. They turned back and followed at a safe distance. But then they got a little more courage.

John was known to the high priest, so he was able to get into the courtyard in front of his house. But Peter had to stay outside. However, John spoke to the servant girl who was on duty at the door, and brought him inside. But just as he was passing in, the girl took a close look at him and said,

'Wait a minute! Aren't you one of his followers?'

But Peter denied it saying,

'I am not.'

Peter went inside and joined a group of people who were gathered around a fire warming themselves because the night was cold. He did his best not to attract attention. However, another servant girl caught a glimpse of his face in the firelight and turned to the others and said,

'This man was with him. I'm sure of it.'

But Peter again denied it saying,

'Woman, I swear I don't even know him.'

Peter thought that they would now leave him alone. But he was mistaken because yet another one of the servants piped up and said,

'You're one of his all right. I saw you in the garden with him tonight. Why, anyone can tell by your accent that you come from Galilee, the same place he comes from.'

Now things were really getting hot for Peter. The man who said this was a servant of the high priest and a relative of Malchus, whose ear he had chopped off. Peter began to curse and swear and said,

'I tell you, I don't even know the man.'

No sooner had he said this than he heard a cock crowing. In a flash the words of Jesus came back to him – 'before the cock crows tomorrow morning, you will have denied me three times.' At that very moment he saw Jesus. He was being taken away, still bound, to Pilate. Jesus looked at Peter. Then Peter knew exactly what he had just done – he had disowned his friend and Master. He felt sick about it. He couldn't stand it inside there any longer. He went outside and wept bitterly.

This was Peter's lowest moment. What saved him from despair was his encounter with Jesus. In that brief and wordless encounter, he realised that not only did Jesus not condemn him, but he actually went on believing in him and loving him. It's an amazing experience to be loved in one's weakness and sinfulness. This is what turned a painful and humbling experience into an hour of grace and salvation.

Judas ends it all

WHEN JUDAS found out that Jesus was going to be killed, he regretted what he had done. Filled with remorse and self-disgust, he brought back the thirty silver pieces to the chief priests. Flinging them down at their feet, he said,

'I have committed a terrible sin. I have betrayed an innocent man.'

But he got no sympathy from them. They just said,

'That's your problem. You deal with it.'

He left them, and instead of trying to come to terms with what he had done, decided to end it all. He went off and hanged himself with a halter. (A halter was a piece of rope used for leading a horse or a donkey.)

The chief priests picked up the money, wondering what to do with it. Then one of them said,

'It wouldn't be right to put it into the collection-box with the offerings of the pilgrims. This is not ordinary money. This is blood money.'

They debated among themselves what to do with it. Finally they decided to buy a piece of land with it. They used the piece of land as a graveyard for strangers.

Peter's denial was not a planned thing, and was the result of weakness rather than malice. Judas' betrayal, on the other hand, was a planned thing, and was carried out in a cold, calculating manner. No one has ever satisfactorily explained what motivated him to do what he did. Like all evil-doers, he is an enigma. It's scary to think that he was exposed to all that Jesus had to offer, yet it came to nothing.

Trial before Pilate

Friday

We've seen how the religious leaders made up their minds that Jesus should be killed. But there was one problem. Only the Romans could pass the death sentence. It was for this reason that they dragged Jesus before Pilate, the Roman Governor.

Pilate had no love for the Jews. They didn't care about him either. But he was afraid to upset the religious leaders, because they could make a lot of trouble for him by stirring up the people against him. Trouble was the last thing his bosses in Rome wanted to hear about. So, whenever he could, Pilate gave in to them for the sake of keeping the peace.

It was still early in the morning when they landed outside his palace with their prisoner. They had Jesus brought into the palace but refused to go in themselves. The reason was this. Pilate was a pagan and a foreigner. Their religion forbade them to enter the house of a foreigner. To do so would make them unclean, and therefore unfit to celebrate the Passover. So Pilate had to go out to meet them.

'What have you got against this man?' he asked.

'Plenty,' they said. 'If he was innocent do you think we would have gone to the trouble of bringing him here?'

'Look, I'd prefer not to get mixed up in this kind of thing,' he said. 'Why can't you take him and judge him according to your own laws?'

'You know very well that we do not have the authority to put a man to death,' they said.

'Oh, so you think he should be put to death. What crime has he committed?' This put them in a spot. The charge of blasphemy (disrespect for God) cut no ice with the Romans. They knew that they would have to come up with a political charge. So they said,

'He has been stirring up trouble among the people. For instance, he has been telling them that he is a king, and that it is wrong to pay taxes to Caesar.'

At this point Pilate went inside to speak to Jesus himself.

'Are you the King of the Jews?' he asked.

'My kingdom is not an earthly kingdom,' Jesus answered. 'My kingdom is a kingdom of truth. It was to speak the truth that I came into the world. Anyone who follows the truth belongs to my Kingdom.'

'What answer do you make to the charges they bring against you?' Pilate asked.

But Jesus didn't answer. Pilate was no dope. He quickly got the message. The charges were ridiculous. Going out to his accusers, he said,

'The man is innocent.'

'He has been stirring up trouble all the way from Galilee to Jerusalem through his teaching,' they insisted.

Convinced that Jesus was innocent, Pilate was looking for a way out for himself. Suddenly he had it. Jesus was from Galilee, which was under Herod's rule. He knew that Herod was in Jerusalem at that time. He would send Jesus to Herod and let him deal with him. This was the same Herod who had killed John the Baptist, and whom Jesus had called 'an old fox'.

Before Herod

HEROD WAS delighted when he heard that Jesus was being brought to him. He had heard a lot about him, and was hoping that maybe he might perform a miracle for him. But Jesus didn't give him any satisfaction. Even though Herod asked him a lot of questions, he refused to answer. Never opened his mouth.

Herod didn't like this. For once he was faced with a man who was not afraid of him. For once he wasn't getting his own way. He got mad. To get his own back on Jesus, he turned his soldiers loose on him. These dressed him up in a king's robe, and made fun of him. But Jesus took it all and still refused to give Herod any answers. In the end, Herod decided to send him back to Pilate.

Before Pilate again

Pilate didn't like to see Jesus coming back to him because he knew it meant trouble for himself. But while he had been with Herod, he had a chance to think things over. He was now more convinced than ever that Jesus was innocent. Being a Roman, he had a sense of justice and fair play. No man should be condemned for something he hadn't done. So he tried for ways to release Jesus.

Having called together the chief priests and leaders of the people, he came out and sat down on his official chair. This meant that he was acting in his capacity as Governor of Judaea. Jesus was standing there in full view, on trial for his life. Then Pilate said,

'You brought this man to me saying that he was leading the people astray. But I have found him to be innocent of the charge. He has done nothing to deserve the death sentence. Therefore, I'll have him whipped and release him.'

But they refused to settle for anything less than the death sentence.

Then Pilate had another idea. It was his custom at Passover time to release a prisoner, someone the people asked for. Now at that time there was a man in prison by the name of Barabbas. He had a terrible record – armed revolt and murder. Pilate said to the people,

'As usual, I'm going to release a prisoner this year. But I'm giving you only two choices: this man here or Barabbas. Who will it be then? Jesus or Barabbas?'

He was full sure they would say, 'Let Barabbas rot, the dirty murderer! Release Jesus to us.'

But the people surprised him. Egged on by the chief priests, they began to chant,

'We want Barabbas! We want Barabbas! '

'What will I do with Jesus?' the Governor asked.

'Crucify him! Crucify him!' they yelled.

Pilate grew more worried than ever. As if things weren't bad enough, at that moment one of his servants brought him a message from his wife. It said: 'This man is innocent. Don't harm him. I had a terrible dream about him last night.' He released Barabbas, and handed Jesus over to his soldiers to be whipped, hoping that this would satisfy the religious leaders.

Whipping, or scourging, was a terrible thing. The victim was stripped to the waist and tied to a pillar. The whip consisted of a club with leather thongs attached to one end. At the end of the thongs, sharp pieces of lead or bones were fixed. These tore the flesh to shreds. It often happened that the victim collapsed and died.

This is what Jesus was now subjected to by Pilate, the coward, who knew he was innocent. Since scourging was done in public, it must have happened right there in the courtyard of Pilate's palace.

The death sentence

You would think that the whipping would have satisfied the soldiers' appetite for pleasure. But it didn't. Afterwards the whole battalion of soldiers gathered around Jesus. They stripped him, and put a purple robe on him. Then they made a crown out of thorns, and pressed it on to his head. Finally they put a reed in his hand. The reed stood for a sceptre, which was a symbol of authority. All this they did to make fun of his claim to be a king.

They took turns in coming in front of him, bowing low like servants before their king. Then they went up to him, took the reed out of his hand, and hit him on the head with it. As they did so, they jeered him, saying,

'Hail, King of the Jews!'

Finally, Pilate called a halt to it, and brought him out, still wearing the crown of thorns and dressed in the purple robe. He put him on display before the people. After they had had a chance to have a good look at him, he said,

'Here he is!'

He was hoping that, having seen the sad state to which he had been reduced, they would take pity on him. But instead they yelled,

'Crucify him! Crucify him!'

'Crucify him yourselves,' Pilate answered. 'As far as I'm concerned, he's an innocent man. Therefore, I'm going to release him.'

The religious leaders couldn't bear the thought of Jesus going free. This was their big chance to get rid of him. They now decided to use another tactic to influence Pilate. It was a thinly-veiled threat.

'If you release this man, you're no friend of Caesar. After all, this man claimed to be a king, which means he's against Caesar.'

On hearing this, Pilate grew scared. He knew that they had him trapped. So he took a bowl of water and washed his hands in front of the people. Then he said,

'My hands are clean. I'm not responsible for this man's death. The responsibility is entirely yours.'

'Let his blood be upon us and upon our children,' they shouted back at him.

Then he handed Jesus over to them to be crucified. The soldiers took the robe off him, and put his own clothes back on him. Then they led him away to the place of execution.

Journey to Skull Hill

Crucifixion was the usual way the Romans executed criminals. The criminal was forced to carry his own cross to the place of execution. He was marched there under an escort of soldiers. One of the soldiers walked in front, carrying a placard on which the man's crime was written. This was later fixed over his head on the cross. They always took the longest route possible. The idea was to let as many people as possible see the condemned man. It was meant to be a warning to them.

All this happened to Jesus. He carried the cross through the narrow streets and lanes of Jerusalem. The 'cross' was probably only the crossbar. The vertical post was usually prepared beforehand at the place of execution. Jesus was so weak that at a certain point they had to force a passer-by to help him with the cross.

The man's name was Simon, and he came from Cyrene in Africa. Simon would not have liked the job. He had come to Jerusalem to celebrate the Passover. It was the chance of a lifetime. Yet here he was carrying the cross of a criminal! However, there is some evidence to suggest that he later became a follower of Jesus. It is known that his two sons, Alexander and Rufus, did. Jesus accepted Simon's help, and no doubt was grateful for it. To see another human being at one's side makes the world seem a friendlier place.

A large crowd followed on behind. Among the crowd was a group of women who were crying. At one point Jesus turned to them and said,

'Don't cry for me. Cry for yourselves and for your children.'

Jesus wasn't rejecting their sympathy. On the contrary, he accepted it and returned it. He knew that Jerusalem would soon know days of terror, and was forewarning the women. It was as if he was saying to them, 'My suffering is nothing compared to what yours will be.'

Pain can so easily turn to rage. This rage may lead us to lash out blindly at whoever happens to be within range. It says a lot, then, about the kind of person Jesus was, that from the depths of his own pain, he could feel for the plight of those women. We will see other examples of this before he died.

There were two other men being executed that day – two thieves. They also were in the procession. At last they reached the place of execution. It was called Calvary, or Skull Hill, and was just outside the city walls. It was still only about nine o'clock in the morning. Some kind women were always on hand to give wine with drugs in it to the condemned men. The idea was to deaden their terrible pain. They offered it to Jesus but he did not drink it.

The Crucifixion

THE SOLDIERS now stripped Jesus once again. This was one further means of degrading and humiliating the condemned person. Besides, to be naked is to be totally vulnerable. Then they nailed his hands and feet to the cross. They did the same to the two thieves. Meanwhile Jesus prayed,

'Father, forgive them. They know not what they do.'

They stood up the three crosses. That was when it hurt most. They put Jesus in the middle, as if he was the chief culprit. Then a placard with his 'crime' was nailed over his head. It had been dictated by Pilate and read: *Jesus of Nazareth, King of the Jews.* It was written in three languages, Hebrew, Greek, and Latin, so that all the strangers who were in the city for the feast would be able to read it.

However, the chief priests didn't like the inscription. They didn't want him as their king. So they went to Pilate and asked him to change it. But he refused to do so. The soldiers who carried out an execution were allowed to take away any of the victim's clothes they fancied. Now Jesus had a good robe and several of them wanted it. So they tossed for it. Having done that, they sat down because they were expected to stay on guard until the condemned men died.

Jesus is mocked

PEOPLE PASSING by now started to jeer and make fun of Jesus. Some said, 'Look at him! The man who said he would pull down the Temple and rebuild it in three days!' Others said,

'If you really are the Son of God, let's see you come down off that cross.'

The chief priests joined in,

'He went around saving other people. Now he can't even save himself. Come down from the cross, and we'll believe in you.'

Even one of the thieves joined in the mockery. He said,

'If you are the Messiah, save yourself and us too.'

But the other thief refused to join in. In fact, he told his comrade off, saying,

'Have you no fear of God? The two of us are guilty, and are only getting what we deserve. But this man is innocent.'

Then he turned to Jesus and said,

'Jesus, remember me when you come into your kingdom.'

And Jesus replied,

'I promise you, this very day you will be with me in Paradise.'

Standing near the cross was a small group of Jesus' friends – his mother, his aunt, Mary Magdalen, and Mary, the wife of Clopas. It must have been very difficult for them, especially for his mother. If only there was something that they could do for him, or say to him, but there wasn't. All they could do was stand there. But by their presence they saved Jesus from dying alone and abandoned.

One of the Twelve was also there, namely John. It seems that Jesus had a soft spot in his heart for John. Now he thought how lonely it was going to be for his mother when he was gone. So he said to her,

'Mother, there is your son.'

And to John he said,

'There is your mother.'

From that day on John took her into his home, and looked after her.

Darkness at noon

Meanwhile a strange darkness came over the land. It began about midday and lasted until Jesus died. This darkness must have added to the anguish of his friends. Time passed slowly. It came on towards three o'clock in the afternoon. Jesus had been hanging there for six hours. Now he made a desperate prayer to his Father. He cried out,

'My God, my God, why have you forsaken me?'

Then he said,

'I'm thirsty.'

One of the soldiers took pity on him, dipped a sponge in a bowl of vinegar, and held it up to his lips and he drank from it. Then he said,

'It is finished.'

And a little while later, he said,

'Father, into your hands I commend my spirit.'

Then he dropped his head and died. It was as simple as that. One minute he was talking. Next minute he was silent.

The Roman officer in charge of the execution had no doubt witnessed many executions in his time. In all probability he was not a religious man. But he was deeply impressed by the way Jesus had died. No sooner had he died than he exclaimed,

'Without a shadow of doubt, this was a good man.'

The burial

WHEN THE Romans crucified people, they left them hanging on the cross until they died. Sometimes people hung there for days, tortured by cold and heat, hunger, thirst, and pain.

However, the next day was the sabbath day – the Passover sabbath. The Jews didn't want to leave the three hanging on the cross during the sabbath, so they went to Pilate and asked him to have their legs broken, so that their bodies could be taken down from the crosses. Pilate gave the go-ahead for this.

The soldiers broke the legs of the two thieves. This was a cruel but quick way of bringing about death. However, when they came to Jesus, they found that he was already dead. But just to make sure, one of them stabbed him in the side with a spear.

The bodies of those who were executed were seldom buried. Usually they were thrown in open ground, to be eaten by the vultures. But this did not happen to the body of Jesus. Two men stepped in to make sure it didn't. The first of these was a man by the name of Joseph from a place called Arimathea. He was a decent man and an important member of the Jewish council – the same council that had plotted the death of Jesus.

Joseph went to Pilate and asked if he could have the body of Jesus. Pilate couldn't believe that he had died so quickly. He sent for the Roman officer and asked him if it was true. The officer said it was. So he allowed Joseph to take away the body. He took it to a tomb in a nearby garden. The tomb was hollowed out of rock, and no one had yet been buried in it.

The second man to step forward was a man we've already met twice – Nicodemus. He also was a member of the Jewish council. It was a Jewish custom to wrap the bodies of the dead in linen cloths and to put sweet spices between the folds of the cloths. It was Nicodemus who provided the cloths. He also provided the spices, enough to bury a king.

They wrapped the body in the linen shroud and laid it in the tomb. Then they closed the tomb by rolling a large stone against its mouth. It was not the kind of farewell they wanted to say. But everything had to be done quickly, because the sabbath rest began at six o'clock.

Darkness fell. Silence wrapped itself around them. A terrible truth began to sink in. He was gone, and it seemed forever. And so they began to grieve.

That's not the end of the story yet. The religious leaders still weren't happy. They went to Pilate and said,

'Your Excellency, we've just remembered something. While this impostor was alive he said, 'After three days I will rise again.' Who's to say that some of his followers won't steal his body, and then go around telling everybody that he has risen from the dead? You know how gullible the people are. They might believe it, and then we would be in a worse position than ever. Don't you think, then, that it would be a good idea to place a guard on his tomb?'

'Go and see to it yourselves,' Pilate answered.

They went and sealed the tomb, and placed a guard of soldiers outside it.

Sad Saturday

ODAY HIS death really hit the apostles. In a sense, today was the day he died. Yesterday had been a day of action. Besides, he was still with them. But today it suddenly dawned on them that he was dead. He was gone. The world seemed so empty without him. They remembered everything good about him. But this served only to bring home to them the enormity of what had happened.

We are not told how they spent the day. Probably hiding in the upper room, with the door locked and the blinds drawn. This was the room in which they had eaten the Last Supper. All was darkness. All was sadness. In times of sorrow some people take refuge in work. However, the apostles couldn't do this because it was the sabbath day.

Meanwhile, the soldiers were standing guard at the tomb. But they seemed strangely out of place, for the sabbath peace lay over all. Inside the tomb lay the body of Jesus. Locked in there with his body were the hopes and dreams of his followers.

An empty tomb

As the run rose on Sunday morning the apostles were still in the grip of sorrow and despair. Shortly after sunrise three women went to the tomb – Mary Magdalen, Mary the mother of James and John, and Salome. They had a very sad task to perform – to complete the embalming of the body of Jesus. For this purpose they had brought along a supply of spices.

As they headed for the tomb one problem worried them. Who would remove for them the huge stone that had been rolled against the mouth of the tomb? But they need not have worried. When they reached the tomb, they were surprised to find that the stone had already been rolled back. They wondered what had happened. Without going into the tomb, they could see that the body was not there. That puzzled them still more.

As soon as Mary Magdalen recovered from the shock, she took off like a hare and ran to Peter and John.

'Someone has taken his body from the tomb,' she blurted out.

'Where have they taken it?' they asked.

'I've no idea,' she replied.

He's alive!

MEANWHILE, the other two women had stayed at the tomb. In fact, they plucked up enough courage to take a peep inside. They were amazed to see a young man sitting there, dressed in a white robe.

'I know that you are looking for Jesus of Nazareth, who was crucified,' he said to them. They nodded faintly. Then he said,

'Why are you looking among the dead for one who is alive? He's not here. He has risen. Look at the place where he was laid. It's empty. Go and take the news to Peter and the others.'

They didn't have to be told twice to get out of there. They ran away from that tomb like people who had seen a ghost. They were so scared that they told no one.

But as we have seen, Mary Magdalen had already spilled the beans about the tomb being empty to Peter and John. The two of these set off at once, and ran to the tomb to see for themselves. John, being a faster runner than Peter, got there first. He looked in through the mouth of the tomb, but did not venture inside. Then Peter arrived, went inside and took a look around. Then John also went inside.

They saw the linen cloths in which Jesus' body had been wrapped lying there, but there was no trace of his body. They couldn't understand it. As yet they were unable to grasp the enormity of what had happened, namely, that Jesus had risen from the dead. Unable to figure it out, they went back home.

Crying by the tomb

MARY MAGDALEN, who had followed them back to the tomb, stayed on there on her own after they left. She took a look inside the tomb and came out again. All this time she was crying. Then she saw a stranger standing there, whom she took to be the gardener.

'Why are you crying?' the stranger asked.

'I'm crying because some people have taken away the body of my Lord, and I don't know where they've put it,' she answered.

Then the stranger said to her,

'Mary.'

Her numbed heart was melted by the warmth in his voice. She took a closer look at him. It was Jesus! She ran up to him, threw herself down in front of him, and hugged his feet. Her tears came faster than ever, only now they were tears of joy. Then he said to her,

'Don't cling to me like that. Instead, go to my disciples and say to them, "I am going to ascend to my Father and to your Father, to my God and to your God." '

Even though she would have loved to stay there with him, she did as he said. She set off at once and went back to Peter and the others, who were still in deep mourning. She burst in on them and said,

'I've seen the Lord!'

But guess what? They didn't believe a word she said. They thought she had imagined the whole thing.

The guards who ran away

WHAT ABOUT the soldiers who were supposed to be guarding the tomb? All we know about them is that at some stage they went and reported what had happened to the chief priests. These didn't like what they heard. This was exactly the kind of thing they had been afraid might happen. They put their heads together and made a quick decision. They decided to bribe the soldiers to lie about what had happened.

'This is what you must tell the people,' they said. 'Say that during the night, while you were asleep, his disciples came and stole the body.'

'But what will Pilate say when he hears that we were sleeping on the job?'

'Don't worry. We'll see to it that you don't get into trouble.'

The soldiers agreed to do as they were asked. They took the money, and that was the story they put out.

Journey to Emmaus

That same evening two of Jesus' disciples were returning to their own village, Emmaus, seven miles north-west of Jerusalem. One of them was Cleopas. We are not given the name of the other one. The two were down in the dumps. They had been full sure that Jesus was the long-awaited Messiah. But when he was killed, all their hopes and dreams went up in smoke.

They went over the events of the previous days again and again. They looked at them from every possible angle, and still couldn't make the slightest sense of them. A crucified Messiah! It was impossible. It was unthinkable. They were walking with their heads cast down. They didn't even lift them when a stranger caught up with them and walked beside them. After a while the stranger said to them,

'You're very sad-looking. What were you talking about just as I joined you?'

'We were talking about the things that happened in Jerusalem during the past few days,' Cleopas answered.

'What things?' he asked.

The question surprised them so they said to him,

'Do you mean to tell us that you haven't heard? You must be the only visitor to Jerusalem who hasn't.'

'Heard about what?' the stranger insisted calmly.

'About Jesus of Nazareth, of course,' said the two. 'He was a man sent by God. Of that there can be no doubt. He did and said great things among the people. But the chief priests arrested him and put him on trial. Then they handed him over to the Romans who crucified him. We firmly believed that he was the Messiah. But obviously we were mistaken because it's three days since all this happened.

'Some women disciples of his gave us a fright. They told us that early this morning they went to his tomb but found it empty. They claimed they saw an angel who told them that he was alive. Those who went to the tomb to check out their story, found that the tomb was indeed empty. But of Jesus himself they saw nothing.'

They lapsed into silence.

'Oh, you foolish men!' the stranger exclaimed. 'You think that because Jesus died like this he couldn't possibly be the Messiah. Haven't you read what the prophets said about the Messiah?'

'We have,' they answered feebly.

'Well then, why didn't you believe them?'

'What do you mean?'

'The prophets foretold that the Messiah would have to suffer and die, and that it would be precisely in this way that he would enter into his glory. How can anyone attain to glory except through sacrifice and suffering?'

'We haven't the remotest idea what you're talking about,' they said.

'Well then, I'll explain myself,' he answered.

Then he explained to them all the parts of the Bible that spoke about the Messiah. He began with Moses and went right through all the prophets, showing them that everything that happened to Jesus had been part of God's plan for the Messiah.

The two listened with rapt attention. So absorbed were they in what he was saying, that they didn't feel the miles going by. Before they knew it, they were in Emmaus. But by this time night was falling. They stopped but he made as if to go on. When they saw this they said to him,

'It's getting late. Why don't you stay here for the night?'

He agreed to do so. Later, when they were having supper, he took the cake of bread, blessed it, broke it, and gave each of them a piece – just as Jesus had done at the Last Supper. Suddenly their eyes were opened and they recognised who the stranger was. It was Jesus himself! But at that moment he disappeared from their sight.

Then they said,

'We should have known all along! Weren't our hearts burning within us as he explained the Bible to us?'

They were so happy and excited that, in spite of the late hour, they set off back the road they had come, all the way to Jerusalem, in order to share the good news with the apostles. When they got back, they found the apostles gathered in the upper room. Then they told them that they had seen Jesus, and reported word for word everything he had said to them. But the eleven weren't really all that surprised to hear what they had to say, because things had been happening for them too – as we will see.

Behind closed doors

THAT EVENING the apostles were gathered in the upper room. However, there were only ten of them present. The two absent ones were Judas and Thomas. We know why Judas wasn't there. As for Thomas – he was off by himself somewhere. He was going through a crisis of faith. Anyway, the ten had the doors of the room securely bolted because they were afraid of the Jews.

While they were having their supper, Jesus appeared among them. They were scared out of their wits. They thought they were seeing a ghost. But he put them at ease when he said,

'Peace be with you! '

They looked and looked but still couldn't believe their eyes. So he said,

'Why are you so frightened? Why all this questioning in your hearts? Look at my hands and my feet. Touch me if you like, and you'll see that it's me. I know you think I'm a ghost. But a ghost doesn't have flesh and bones as I have.'

When he had said this, he showed them his hands and his feet. They were overcome with joy, but still found it hard to believe. Knowing this, he said,

'I can see that you still don't believe. Well then, have you anything to eat?'

They gave him a bit of grilled fish. He took it and ate it right in front of them. That seemed to do the trick. Then he said,

'Peace be with you. The Father sent me into the world on a mission. I am sending you into the world to carry on that same mission.'

Then, breathing on them, he said,

'Receive the Holy Spirit. If you forgive the sins of anyone, then God will count them forgiven also. If you retain the sins of anyone, God will retain them also.'

Having said these things, he left them as mysteriously as he had come.

And so the day came to a close. What a day it had been! Their tears had been turned into laughter, their despair into hope. They began to believe and hope again. No wonder that later on, when they cut their ties with the Jewish religion, they changed their holy day from Saturday to Sunday – the day Jesus broke the chains of death and rose in triumph from the grave.

The mark of the nails

Thomas eventually showed up. As soon as he appeared, they cried out excitedly,

'We've seen the Lord!'

But he wasn't impressed. He just said,

'Unless I can put my finger into the mark of the nails, and put my hand into the spear wound in his side, I won't believe.'

No matter how hard they tried, they couldn't convince him.

A week later they were gathered once more

in the same room. This time Thomas was with them. They were still taking no chances, and had the door bolted as firmly as ever. But bolts and locks could not keep out the risen Jesus. Before they knew what was happening, he was standing in the midst of them. They were scared, especially Thomas.

'Peace be with you,' Jesus said.

On hearing this, all except Thomas relaxed a little. He just couldn't believe his eyes. But then Jesus came right up to him and said,

'Thomas, look at my hands. See the mark of the nails. And look at my side. See the spear wound.'

Thomas looked and saw. Then Jesus said to him,

'Now, put your finger into the nail marks, and put your hand into the spear wound. See for yourself that I'm real. Then stop all this doubting and believe.'

Thomas did as the Lord told him. He put his finger into the wounds in the hands of Jesus. He put his hand into the hole in his side left by the spear. In truth, Thomas too was wounded. But while Jesus' wounds were visible, Thomas' wounds were invisible. He was wounded by doubt and grief. But when he touched the wounds of Jesus, his own wounds were healed.

'You are my Lord and my God!' he cried.

And Jesus said,

'Thomas, you believe in me because you have seen me and touched me. But blessed are those who believed without having to see or touch me.'

This was a little dig at Thomas' stubbornness. But it was also meant as an encouragement for us who are asked to believe without being able to see or touch Jesus.

Nevertheless, we can sympathise with Thomas. He was merely echoing the human cry for certainty. However, here on earth there is no absolute certainty about spiritual things. If there was, then faith would not be necessary.

Fish for breakfast

Once Jesus appeared, not in Jerusalem, but by the sea of Galilee. It happened like this. One evening Peter said to the others,

'I'm going fishing. Any of you care to join me?'

Six of them did – James, John, Thomas, Bartholomew, and two others. They got into the boat, rowed out, and began to fish. They fished all night long but caught nothing. As dawn was breaking they decided to call it a night, so they pulled in the net and headed back to shore. As they neared the shore, they saw a man standing there, but didn't take much notice of him until he called to them.

'Catch anything, friends?' he asked.

'Not a thing,' they replied glumly.

Then he said,

'Have one more go. Right there where you are.'

He said this in such a way that they obeyed him at once. They let down the net and made a large catch of fish. John remembered that this had happened before. He looked closely at the stranger on the shore, and then exclaimed,

'It's the Lord!'

When Peter heard this he couldn't wait any longer. Leaving the others to bring in the boat and the fish, he tucked up the few rags he was wearing, jumped overboard and waded ashore. Jesus had a fire going. Bread and fish lay beside it. He asked them if they would like a little breakfast. They said they would. Then he said,

'Bring some of the fish you've just caught, and we'll see what they taste like.'

Peter went back on board and hauled the net up on to the beach. It was a miracle it didn't break because it contained 153 large fish – this time it was the little ones that got away. Then he picked out a few of them and gave them to Jesus. He cooked them, and when everything was ready he said,

'Sit down now and have something to eat.'

The boys were only too glad to oblige. As they sat there eating, they were absolutely certain that it really was Jesus. Yet none of them had the courage to say so to his face.

After breakfast Jesus turned to Peter. Peter guessed that something was coming. He was probably expecting a telling-off. He was afraid Jesus might say something like,

'You're some friend! That was a nice thing you did to me on Thursday night. Not once, but three times, you swore before all those people that you didn't know me. You're nothing but a coward. I'm finished with you.'

But he was completely wrong, because Jesus said,

'Peter, do you love me more than these others love me?'

Peter was so surprised that for a while he couldn't say anything. But then he said,

'Yes, Lord, I do.'

And Jesus said,

'Feed my lambs.'

Peter felt very relieved. It was a lovely feeling to be trusted again, especially after he had made such a mess of things.

Then Jesus asked him a second time,

'Peter, do you love me?'

'Yes, Lord, I do love you,' Peter answered.

'Feed my sheep,' Jesus said.

That made Peter feel even better. But then Jesus asked him a third time,

'Peter, do you love me?'

Now Peter got very upset. Did Jesus not believe him? Finally he said,

'Lord, you know all things. Well then, you must know that I love you.'

And Jesus said to him,

'Feed my lambs. Feed my sheep.'

Not only did Jesus not discard Peter, but there were no recriminations either. He knew that Peter really did love him. Love and weakness can and do coexist in the same human heart. Jesus asked him to declare his love in public, since his denials had also been in public.

Peter felt good again. He understood that Jesus was putting him in charge of his entire flock. He was being asked to take the place of Jesus himself. No small task! Jesus was the Good Shepherd, who gave his life for his sheep. One day Peter would be asked to do the same. But he didn't know that yet.

Last instructions and goodbye

Jesus made many more appearances to the apostles over a period of forty days. During the last one he gave them some very important instructions. He said,

'I have been given authority over the whole world. Now I'm sharing that authority with you. Go out into the whole world. Preach the Gospel to everyone. Teach them everything I taught you. Baptise them in the name of the Father, and of the Son, and of the Holy Spirit. And remember this: I will be with you always, right to the end of time. However, don't start just yet. Wait until I send you the Holy Spirit as I promised. Stay in the city until you receive power and strength from him.'

Having said this, he led them out of the city and up to the top of the Mount of Olives. When they reached the top, he stood and looked around at them. These were the people who would continue the work he had started. In a sense everything now depended on them. He blessed them, and then was lifted up in front of their eyes. Up he went until a cloud hid him from view, and they saw him no more.

They continued to stand there for some time gazing up into the sky. But then a voice from nearby brought them back to earth. Two men dressed in white robes were standing there. One of them said,

'Men of Galilee, why are you standing there looking up into the sky? Jesus, whom you have seen being taken up into heaven, will come back again in the same way.'

No doubt this gave them hope. It also helped them to understand what had happened. Jesus had gone back to his Father, to take his place at his right hand in the heavenly kingdom. He had earned the right to sit in that place of honour, because he had carried out his Father's mission faithfully.

Even though they were saddened by his leaving, they were happy at the thought that he had gone to his glory. They would no longer be able to see him, because he wouldn't be physically present with them. But they believed that he would be with them in other ways, as he said he would.

So they pulled themselves together and returned to the city in good spirits. They went straight to the upper room. There they spent their time praying and waiting for the coming of the Holy Spirit. They left the room once a day to visit the Temple. All eleven apostles were there. Jesus' mother, Mary, was also there, as well as a number of other women.

Picking a sub for Judas

ONE DAY they held a big meeting. There were about 120 people at it. Peter got up to speak. 'Friends,' he said, 'I've got something important to discuss with you. You all know that Jesus chose twelve of us to be his apostles. But we are now reduced to eleven. Judas is no longer with us. Everybody knows how he betrayed the Lord. And see what a sad and wretched end he came to!

'However, since he departed the scene there has been a vacancy. I think the time has come for us to fill that vacancy. We must pick someone to take the place of Judas. In my view the person we pick must be someone who, like Judas, was with us ever since we first met the Lord Jesus. But what do you think?'

Everybody thought this was a good idea. Then they nominated two candidates, both of whom were considered to be highly suitable for the post. The names of the two were Joseph and Matthias. Since only one was needed, they had to choose between them. Before making their choice they prayed to God for guidance. Their payer went like this:

'Lord, you can read the hearts of all people. We ask you now to look into the hearts of these two men, and show us which of them you want to take the place left vacant by Judas.'

Then they put the two names into a hat, and got someone to pick one of them out. Out came the name of Matthias. From that day on he was called an apostle like the other eleven.

Wind and fire

Nine days after Jesus had left them was the feast of Pentecost. This was an important Jewish feast. It was really a harvest festival, during which they offered to God the first-fruits of their crops. It turned out to be a red-letter day for the apostles, because this was the day Jesus kept his promise to send them the Holy Spirit.

On that day they were all gathered in the upper room as usual. They were praying and everything was nice and quiet. Suddenly they heard the sound of a mighty wind. The roaring of it filled the whole house and must have frightened the daylights out of them. They probably thought that the house was about to collapse on top of them.

As if that wasn't bad enough, fire appeared. Tongues of fire came down on the head of each of them. Yet none of them got burned. No harm came to them from the wind either. In fact, something tremendous happened to them. They were filled with the Holy Spirit, and then all heaven broke loose.

Up to this they were weak and cowardly. They were afraid to speak out. They didn't seem to be able to get going. They were like sail boats waiting for the wind. Now, however, the Holy Spirit took hold of them, as if to say,

'Come on! Look alive! You've been hiding long enough in this room. It's high time you went out of here, and began to speak about Jesus to the people.'

At any rate, they suddenly found their tongues. They began to speak, not only in their own native language, but in several foreign languages as well. They went out of that room full of courage, afraid of no one. They were like people on fire – on fire with love for Jesus, their risen Lord.

Friends, lend us your ears

THERE WERE people in Jerusalem from all over the Middle East for the feast, and they spoke several different languages. The apostles now began to preach boldly to these. The people were amazed that they could understand what they were saying. They couldn't figure out how simple men from Galilee were able to speak their languages.

'How do they manage it?' they asked one another.

But none of them could explain how. However, some cynics said,

'The explanation is simple. They've been drinking too much new wine, and it has gone to their heads. It's the wine that's talking.'

Then Peter, with the rest of the Twelve at his side, stood up and made a speech to the people.

'Listen, all of you,' he said. 'These men are not drunk. It's far too early in the day for that. It's only nine o'clock. It's not the wine that's talking in these men but the Holy Spirit. This is what the prophet Joel was talking about when he said:

When the Lord's great day dawns,
wonderful things will happen.
Your young people will see visions.
Your old folk will dream dreams.
On that day the Lord will pour out his Spirit on all the people.
Everyone who calls on God for help will be saved.

'Fellow Jews, I appeal to you to give us a hearing. We want to tell you the truth about Jesus of Nazareth. He was a man near and dear to God. You can tell that by the miracles he did among you. You killed this good man. And God didn't stop you. He allowed Jesus to taste death. But God did not allow Jesus to rot in the grave. He loved him too much to allow that to happen. He raised him up to life. We know this for a fact because we have seen him alive.

'Not only has God raised him to life again, but he has also promoted him. He has made him his right-hand man in his Kingdom. He is sitting there now in all his glory. It was from there that he sent the Holy Spirit on us as he told us he would. What you are witnessing is an outpouring of that Spirit. All this has happened to show you that God has made Jesus, whom you crucified, both Lord and Christ.' (Lord meant that Jesus was divine; Christ meant he was the Messiah.)

Many of those present believed Peter. Suddenly it dawned on them what a rotten thing they had done to Jesus. They wanted to make amends. So they asked,

'What should we do, brothers?'

'The first thing you must do is turn away from your sins,' Peter replied. 'Next you must be baptised in the name of Jesus. Then you too will receive the gift of the Holy Spirit.'

Peter went on talking like that, and guess what? By the end of the day, about three thousand people had accepted baptism and become believers in Jesus.

A new way of living

THESE FIRST believers threw themselves into the Christian way of life with all their hearts. They took all their teaching from the apostles. They tried to live as close friends. They shared everything they owned so that no one went in need of anything. They were closely united among themselves. In a word, they loved and cared for one another just as Jesus said his disciples should.

They didn't neglect their prayers either. Every day they continued to go in groups to the Temple. They also met in each other's houses to pray and to break bread. (To *break bread* was how they referred to what Jesus did at the Last Supper. In time this was called the Eucharist, or the Mass.) They lived such good lives that many people admired them.

They didn't follow their own selfish desires. That would have led to such things as: adultery, feuds, quarrels, jealousies, outbursts of anger, drunkenness, and so on. These are ugly things which make life miserable.

Instead they followed the lead of the Spirit, and these are the things they received in their lives: love, joy, peace, patience, kindness, goodness, trustfulness, gentleness and self-control. These are known as the fruits of the Holy Spirit. They are beautiful things which make life wholesome and joyful.

Those feet were meant for walking

SOON THE apostles began to cure people, and this made them even better known. For instance, one evening Peter and John were going into the Temple to say their prayers. A cripple was sitting there on the steps begging. His friends used to leave him there in the morning, and call back for him in the evening. The man had been crippled from birth, and was now over forty years old .

'Could you spare a few coppers?' the man asked.

Peter and John stopped and, looking at him, felt sorry for him. Feet, after all, are meant for walking, not sitting on. So Peter said to him,

'Look at me.'

The man did so, thinking that he was going to get some money. But Peter said,

'I've no money to give you, my friend, but I've something better.'

'What's that?' he asked.

'Would you like to be able to walk?'

'Of course I would.'

'Well then, do as I tell you. In the name of Jesus of Nazareth, get up and walk.'

'Walk? I can't even stand!' the man exclaimed.

'Let me help you,' said Peter.

Peter helped him up onto his shaky feet. The poor chap got a terrible fit of the wobbles. But then somehow his ankles got stronger. He took a step, and then another. Peter then let go of him, and he was able to manage on his own. Once he knew he could make it, there was no holding him. He began to hop and dance around the place, out of his mind with joy. Then he went into the Temple with them, all the time walking and jumping and praising God.

The people who were there at the time, and who had known the crippled man, were overcome with amazement. They couldn't figure out how all of a sudden he was able to walk. There was a lot of excitement. A large crowd gathered. When Peter saw the crowd he grabbed the opportunity to make a speech about Jesus.

He said,

'Friends, I know that you are wondering how it is that this man, who never walked in his life, is now able to walk. You are looking at us as though we had cured him. This man owes his cure, not to us, but to Jesus of Nazareth.'

'But Jesus is dead,' they answered. 'We killed him.'

'So you did,' said Peter, 'and a rotten death you gave him. First of all you handed him over to Pilate. When he wanted to release him, what did you do? You turned around and asked for the release of a murderer, Barabbas, instead. You let a murderer go free, and killed the very author of life itself! But God raised him from the dead. Jesus is alive. We are witnesses to that fact. It is through faith in Jesus that this man is able to walk.'

They were amazed to hear all this. They realised that they had indeed given Jesus a raw deal, and felt bad about it. Knowing how they were feeling, Peter said,

'Now I believe that neither you nor the religious leaders really knew what you were doing when you crucified Jesus. Besides, God has brought good out of it. This was how what the prophets said about the Messiah having to suffer came true. Jesus is the Messiah. The promises God made to our ancestors through the prophets are being fulfilled in our times.'

Stop this preaching, or else!

Before Peter could finish his speech, the Temple guards arrived on the scene. They had been sent by the priests who were raging with the apostles because they were teaching the people that Jesus was risen from the dead. The guards arrested Peter and John. However, since it was late in the day, they didn't question them there and then. Instead, they put them in jail overnight.

Next morning the Jewish leaders called a meeting in the presence of Caiphas, the high priest. They brought Peter and John from the jail, and began to question them. But the two were well able to defend themselves, something which baffled the leaders.

'By what power, and by whose name, did you cure this man?' they asked.

'Through the name of Jesus of Nazareth, the man you crucified,' Peter answered boldly.

'But he's dead.'

'No he's not. He's alive.'

'Nonsense!'

'God raised him from the dead. He is like a stone which you, the builders, rejected. But now God has made him the foundation stone of a new building. In fact, his is the only name in all the world by which we can be saved.'

The argument went on. But the one fact that no one could deny was that a miracle had happened, because the man himself was standing there before their eyes. He was standing on his own two pins, as straight and steady as a sentry on duty. At a certain point they removed Peter and John from the room so that they could discuss what to do with them in private.

'What are we going to do?' they asked. 'The whole of Jerusalem knows about the miracle by now.'

'We must stop it from going any further,' someone said. 'We must tell them that from now on they must not speak or teach in the name of Jesus.'

'Why don't we give them a good hiding,' another suggested. 'Then they'll stop this preaching lark.'

'That would not be wise,' a leader answered. 'It could lead to trouble among the people, who seem to have been completely carried away by what they have done. For the moment at least we must leave it at a warning.'

So they brought them back into the room and said,

'Look, you must stop your preaching. You must stop it at once.'

'Is that an order?' asked Peter.

'It is, and you had better take it seriously,' came the answer.

'We can't obey an order like that,' John said. 'We believe that God himself is ordering us to continue preaching. Obedience to God comes first.'

They warned them once again, this time in even sterner tones, and then released them.

Did they keep quiet? No way. They preached all the more about Jesus. Besides, they performed many cures in his name. People came in crowds from the towns around Jerusalem, bringing their sick with them, and the apostles cured them all. Peter, especially, was in great demand. People went home happy if even his shadow fell on them as he went past.

Arrested again

When the high priest and his friends heard about this they were raging. Once again they arrested them and threw them into prison, right in with common criminals. But during the night an angel came to their rescue. We are not told whether it was an angel with wings or just with feet. The main thing is that he was good at picking locks, because he opened the gates of the prison and let the apostles out.

They didn't head for the hills or go into hiding. At dawn they went straight to the temple and began to preach there. When the chief priests found out what had happened, they sent some temple guards to arrest them, and bring them in for further questioning. But they warned them not to use violence in case the people might stone them.

So once again the apostles had to face the high priest and his friends. This time these were not prepared to take any nonsense. The high priest began,

'We warned you to stop preaching about Jesus. But instead of doing as you were told, you have gone and preached about him to every Tom, Dick and Harry. To make matters worse, you are putting all the blame for his death on us. What have you got to say for yourselves?'

'Obedience to God comes before obedience to people,' they answered. 'You can't deny that it was you who had Jesus executed by hanging him on a tree. But as we said before, God has raised him up. We are witnesses to that fact. Now he sits at God's right hand in glory. He is our Leader and Saviour. All who believe in him can have their sins forgiven.'

On hearing this they were furious and wanted to kill them on the spot. But a man called Gamaliel, a decent man, intervened. He asked that the apostles be taken out of the room for a while. Then he said,

'Let's not kill them. We don't want blood on our hands. I've got a better idea. Let's leave them carry on with what they're doing. If it's God's work, as they claim it is, it will succeed in spite of us. If it is the work of the devil, it will eventually collapse of its own accord.'

Everybody thought that this was a good solution to the problem. Nevertheless, having called the apostles back in, they gave orders for them to be flogged. Then having warned them that worse would follow if they didn't stop preaching about Jesus, they released them.

You might think that this would have made the apostles go away licking their wounds and feeling sorry for themselves. Not at all. They went away in high spirits, delighted that they had been given a chance to suffer for Jesus, who had suffered and died for them. Nor did this stop them preaching. If anything it had the opposite effect. They went on preaching about Jesus every day, both in the Temple and in private houses.

The first deacons

B Y NOW THE number of disciples had increased greatly. Wherever you have human beings, you have problems. The early Christian community was no exception. It too experienced problems. One of these problems concerned the daily distribution of food to widows. Some people complained that the widows were being neglected. So the apostles called a general meeting of all the disciples, and addressed them as follows:

'It would not be right for us to neglect the preaching of the word of God in order to give out food. So what we suggest is this. You must choose from among yourselves seven men of good reputation, filled with the Holy Spirit and with wisdom. Then we will hand the task of distributing food over to them. That will leave us free to devote ourselves to prayer and to preaching.'

The whole assembly approved of this. The seven men they selected were: Stephen, Philip, Prochorus, Nicanor, Timon, Parmenas and Nicolaus. They presented these to the apostles. The apostles ordained them deacons by praying over them and laying their hands on them. A deacon is someone who serves the community

The first martyr

N OW STEPHEN, one of the seven deacons, was full of faith and courage. And he was well able to argue the case for Jesus with the Jews. But some of them got jealous of him and had him arrested. They paid some creeps to claim that they had heard him say that Jesus would destroy the Temple, and do away with the traditions handed down by Moses.

Stephen was brought before the high priest and his Council. The high priest asked him if the charge was true. Stephen denied the charge. But they pressed him and pressed him so that he began to argue with them. The argument went on for a long time. He tried to prove to them from the Bible that Jesus was the Messiah. But eventually, realising that he was getting nowhere, he lost his cool and said,

'You people are as stubborn as mules! You are worse than the pagans! You persecuted every single prophet that God sent to you. Every one of those prophets spoke about the Holy One who was to come into the world. And when at last he came in the person of Jesus, what did you do? You killed him. Just think of it! You killed God's Holy One!'

On hearing this they began to froth at the mouth with rage. But Stephen went on,

'I'm not afraid of you. At this very moment I can see Jesus standing at God's right hand in glory.'

That was the limit. They could take no more. They rushed at him and dragged him out of the city, and stoned him to death. As he died Stephen prayed,

'Lord Jesus, receive my spirit. Do not hold this sin against them.'

When he was dead his killers took away his clothes, and handed them over to a man called Saul. Saul told them that they had done a good day's work in getting rid of Stephen. Some of Stephen's friends came and took away his mangled body and buried it.

Saul really hated the Christians – that's what the followers of Jesus were now called. He was fully determined to get rid of every single one of them. He went around searching houses. Whenever he found any of them, he dragged them out and flung them into prison.

Why did Saul hate the Christians so much? He was a fanatical Pharisee. Jesus had numerous clashes with the Pharisees, and they played a big part in his death. Saul saw the followers of Jesus as a threat to his kind of religion, which was highly orthodox and extremely traditional. Hence, he feared them. Fear easily turns into hate. But then he had an experience which turned him from being a bitter enemy of Jesus into one of his greatest apostles.

Seeing the light

ONE DAY HE set out for the town of Damascus with a list of the Christians who lived there. He was determined to arrest them, and bring them back to Jerusalem for trial. He set out, feeling very sure of himself. He was within sight of Damascus when the incident occurred. All of a sudden there came a blinding flash of light. He fell to the ground. As he was lying there, he heard a voice saying to him,

'Saul, Saul, why are you persecuting me?'

'Who are you?' he asked in a trembling voice.

'I am Jesus, and you are persecuting me.'

Saul made no answer to this. Then Jesus said to him,

'Get up off the ground, and go into the town. There you will be told what to do.'

When Saul stood up he got another shock, even worse than the first one. He was as blind as a bat. He felt so helpless that somebody had to take him by the hand, and lead him in to the town. His blindness lasted for three days. During that time he didn't eat or drink anything.

Meanwhile, in Damascus, a disciple by the name of Ananias had a vision. In it he too heard Jesus talking to him.

'Ananias,' Jesus said.

'Here I am, Lord,' he answered.

'Go at once to the house of Judas in Straight Street,' Jesus said. 'When you get there, ask for a man by the name of Saul.'

'Hold on, Lord,' Ananias replied. 'Surely you don't mean the Saul who is going around persecuting your followers?'

'The very man,' said Jesus.

'Well, in that case, I don't want anything to do with him.'

'He won't harm you. He's blind. But I want you to go and pray over him, so that he may get his sight back.'

'Leave him as he is, Lord. That way he won't be able to harm your followers.'

'Believe me, you will see a changed Saul. I have big plans for the same Saul. I have chosen him to make my name known among the Gentiles. He will suffer an awful lot for my sake, but he doesn't know that yet.'

On hearing this Ananias changed his mind and went.

When he found Saul he said to him,

'Saul, my brother, Jesus has sent me to you. He wants you to have your sight back, and to receive the Holy Spirit.'

This was music to Saul's ears. He knelt down, and Ananias put his hands on his head and began to pray over him. Immediately a kind of film fell from his eyes, and he was able to see again. He was baptised on the spot. Only then would he have something to eat. As soon as he had eaten, he regained his strength.

The experience changed Saul. To show how changed he was, he took a new name, Paul – the name by which he has been known ever since. Believe it or not, after a few days he began to preach in the local synagogues that Jesus was the Messiah. The people who had known him before were amazed at the change that had come over him. They asked one another,

'Can this really be the same man who carried out organised attacks on the followers of Jesus in Jerusalem? Can this be the man who came here for the sole purpose of arresting those same followers who live here?'

It was indeed hard to believe it, but Paul himself left them in no doubt. Then some of them rounded on him, calling him a turn-coat and a traitor. But he stood up to them and was more than a match for any of them when it came to debating about Jesus. In fact, he threw the whole Jewish community at Damascus into confusion.

Pretty soon things took a nasty turn. His enemies drew up a to plan to kill him. The result was that Paul had to go into hiding. His enemies kept watch at the gates of the town in case he tried to slip out unknownst to them. But with a little help from his friends Paul succeeded in outwitting his enemies. One dark night they let him down over the wall in a basket, and he escaped to Jerusalem.

Even in Jerusalem many of the disciples were suspicious of him. But then a disciple by the name of Barnabas came to his aid. He introduced him to the apostles. Once they accepted that his conversion was genuine, things improved for him.

He was able to begin preaching about Jesus in Jerusalem. And he did so with such enthusiasm and courage that here too he soon made some of the Jews mad. Once again his life was in danger, and once again he had to flee. His friends smuggled him out of the city and took him to Caesarea. From there he went on to Tarsus, which was his home town.

The end of the beginning

THAT'S HOW PAUL got started on his work for the Lord. After this he went around, mostly among the Gentiles, founding little groups of believers in places like Corinth, Ephesus, Colossae and Rome. Since he could only be in one place at a time, he got the idea of writing letters to the various churches (groups of disciples) he had founded. In these letters he dealt with their problems, and encouraged them to persevere in the faith.

He did wonderful work in spreading the Gospel in the non-Jewish world, but paid a big price for his success. It is doubtful if anyone ever endured as much as he endured. He wasn't a man to boast, but in one of his letters he tells us about some of his trials:

I have been imprisoned.

I have been whipped, almost to the point of death.

Three times I was beaten with sticks.

Once I was stoned and left for dead. (By 'stoned' he doesn't mean high on drugs or booze.)

Three times I was shipwrecked.

Once I spent a day and a night adrift in the open sea.

I have travelled thousands of miles on foot, often narrowly escaping death at the hands of robbers or enemies.

I have worked like a dog, often right through the night.

I've known hunger and thirst.

I've known freezing cold and nakedness.

And on top of all these sufferings I've carried the burden of worry and concern for all the churches. (2 Cor 11:23-29).

Meanwhile, Peter and the others hadn't been idle either. Things got so hot for them in Jerusalem that they were forced to spread out. This was not a bad thing because everywhere they went, they preached the Gospel, and set up little communities of believers like Paul did.

That's how the great adventure of Christianity got started. Ever since then it has gone on spreading. The followers of Jesus have been carrying out the final command he gave them: 'Preach the Gospel to the whole world.' The word Gospel means Good News.

Unfortunately, those followers haven't always behaved as Christians should. There have been bitter quarrels among them, with the result that today we have not one Christian Church, but several Christian Churches. Yet, in spite of the failings of his followers, and many terrible persecutions, the Gospel has come down to us across two thousand years. The explanation for this surely lies in the promise of Jesus: 'I will be with you always, to the very end of time.'

APPENDIX
Maps

PALESTINE

IN

THE TIME OF CHRIST

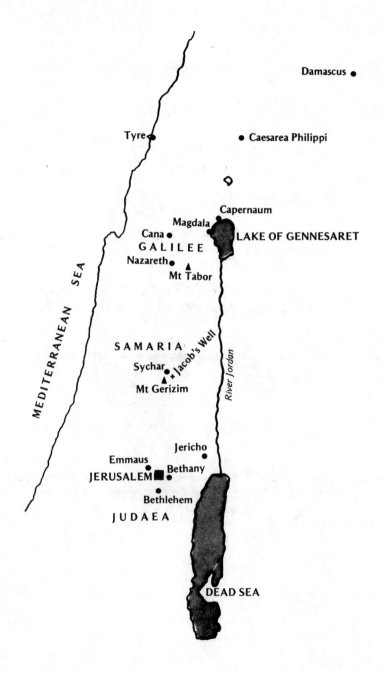

Damascus •

Tyre •

• Caesarea Philippi

Capernaum •

Magdala •

Cana •

LAKE OF GENNESARET

G A L I L E E

Nazareth •

▲ Mt Tabor

MEDITERRANEAN   SEA

S A M A R I A

Jacob's Well

Sychar •

+

River Jordan

▲

Mt Gerizim

Jericho •

Emmaus •

Bethany

JERUSALEM ■

Bethlehem •

J U D A E A

DEAD SEA

JERUSALEM

IN

THE TIME OF CHRIST

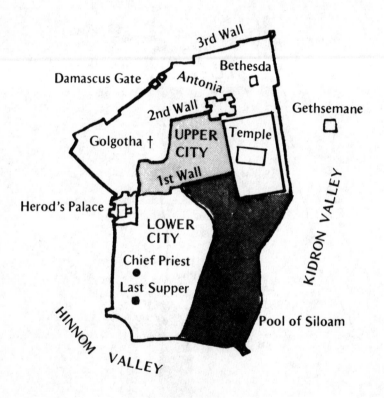

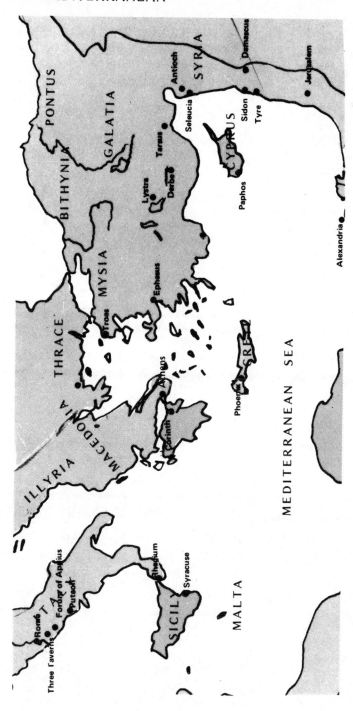